Food & Trembling

Food & Trembling

An Entertainment

Jonah Campbell

Invisible Publishing

Halifax & Toronto

Library and Archives Canada Cataloguing in Publication

Campbell, Jonah, 1981-
    Food and trembling : an entertainment / Jonah Campbell.

Includes index.
Issued also in electronic format.
ISBN 978-1-926743-15-8

    1. Gastronomy. 2. Food. 3. Food--Humor. I. Title.

TX631.C36 2011   641.01'3   C2011-905796-4

Cover & interior illustrations by Geordan Moore

Typeset in Laurentian and Gibson by Megan Fildes
Special thanks to type designer Rod McDonald

Printed and bound in Canada

Invisible Publishing
Halifax & Toronto
www.invisiblepublishing.com

We acknowledge the support of the Canada Council for the Arts which last
year invested $20.1 million in writing and publishing throughout Canada.

Invisible Publishing recognizes the support of the Province of Nova Scotia
through the Department of Communities, Culture & Heritage. We are
pleased to work in partnership with the Culture Division to develop and
promote our cultural resources for all Nova Scotians.

NOVA SCOTIA
Tourism, Culture and Heritage

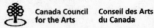

Canada Council   Conseil des Arts
for the Arts   du Canada

For Barbara.

"In my youth I was always taught that you should take a woman by the waist and a bottle by the neck."

"I am glad you told me. I shall continue to hold a bottle by the waist and give women a wide berth."

–W. Somerset Maugham,
Ashenden, or, The British Agent

A Note on the Definitions

All definitions are drawn from the *Compact Edition of the Oxford English Dictionary* (Oxford, 1971) which at 4,134 pages, four microphotographed original pages per, provides a wealth of entertainment to those inclined toward, er, dusty and obscure deipnographs. It was originally Ammon Shea's *Reading the OED* (2008) that set me off on this pursuit, and I owe the discovery of some terms to his Herculean efforts. In such cases, however, I made a point of following up on the original entry myself, and all commentary is my own.

Part One: Eat to Live

A Condiment is a Condiment is a Condiment. Is a Condiment a Condiment?

or
I Drank a Lot of Scotch Last Night and Woke Up to Find This on My Computer

Condiment, *noun* Anything of pronounced flavour used to season or give relish to food, or to stimulate the appetite. Hence ~al. [f. L *condimentum* (*condire* – pickle)]

I just ate what probably would have been the best sandwich of my life, had I not already eaten such a sandwich numerous times over the course of the past two and seven-tenths of a decade, and that is largely the point—it was not merely a delicious sandwich, but a sandwich that conjures in the mind and on the palate a whole history of sandwiches that each tasted more or less the same and each imparted a comparable sense of satisfaction and well-being. A sandwich that draws upon a strong lineage.

I speak, of course, of the BLT.

More or less. It's been a long time since I've eaten bacon, my lapses and furtive forays into carnivory notwithstanding, but it lives on in vivid, defiant, seductive detail in my tongue's brain's heart—a sort of over-saturated image of a myth of a meat. And it's gotten me thinking about:

1. The vegetarian BLT, and how it is that a creature lacking in bacon could, and can, and still continues to, *feel* like a

BLT, in the face even of the acknowledgement that a similar sandwich lacking in tomato or lettuce would never come across as convincingly BLT-like (sometimes one tries to reproduce the bacon with tempeh or tofu or smoky-maple tofu or smoked coconut or something, but sometimes one contents oneself with sautéed onions, an appropriate amount of black pepper, and soy sauce, and doesn't feel particularly short-shrifted for it).

2. The often unsung roles of condiments in said mix— for example, I don't know that it's universal, but a BLT without mayonnaise (or a reasonable facsimile) is an ersatz, and probably loathsomely dry affair in my books. Furthermore, and this is probably pushing it, the ideal sandwich should also involve some margarine, but I grant that perhaps with actual bacon the fragile of spirit might think that unnecessary.

Fortunately I don't really care about the answer to this question, I care merely about deliciousness.

Thus, deliciousness:

Bread (turned into toast, probably, but not necessarily.)

One small onion, sliced and sautéed with salt & black pepper, possibly just a little soy sauce, putting about ten-percent aside to leave raw, for bite.

Tomato, sliced.

Lots of lettuce. At the moment I prefer romaine, but really

anything will do. It's nice to have something with at least a bit of crunch, so maybe iceberg or any leafier beast close to the base.

Margarine.

Mayonnaise. Lots. What are you, a giant baby?

A diplomatic and restrained application of almond butter (Or in a pinch—tahineh, less still).

A dusting of nutritional yeast (*in* the sandwich, I mean). Possibly some hot sauce, usually as an afterthought, usually of a simple constitution. This always tastes like a BLT to me, or, like a summons to all my foolish blood, at least produces the BLT-marked endorphin profile that feels like a hug to the heart; even without the almond butter and nutritional yeast and hot sauce, or possibly with a little prepared mustard. Fuck, I don't know, it's your sandwich.

But why BLT in lieu of, say, MLT? Why does this distinctly remain a BLT when I have proven to myself that mayo is of greater importance than the bacon?

Why does the condiment silently suffer relegation to the status of invisibility in flagrant disregard of the essential work that it performs? In point of fact, what really is the distinction between ingredient and condiment (**Ingredient, adjective.** Component part, element, in a mixture. [f. L *gredi*/gress = *gradi* step])? Why does the condiment carry such an air of the incidental in contrast to the supposed consequentiality (for the framing/naming of a dish) of the so-called ingredients?

I demand answers. No justice, no peace.

In Which Two Edith Wharton Characters Admit to Mutual and Increasingly Shattering Betrayals

I would like to say that there are food experiences I will never forget, but we know that memory does not work that way. Or *we*, to say the least, do not work that way. Memory is coloured and discoloured as it weathers with age, now losing lustre, now gaining wholly original hues, and is altogether a fickle and transient critter, serving ends sadly unknowable to the rest of us. We being the possessors (or awful products!) of such critters.

Strange that I unthinkingly used only language of colour, despite talking about taste (although I have been thinking about Nabokov a lot lately).

In all likelihood, just as I distrust my ability to recall from the past the exact details of a scene or conversation or piece of music, so too do I presume my remembered tastes to be mostly fabulation. For it's not as if I can truly conjure the taste again in my mouth, however popular this idea is in Western literature, gastronomical or otherwise. Not to be misunderstood—I do not cast aspersions on the claims of others, but I have no such confidence in the fidelity of my own memory. Of course the meat of the thing (memory) is not total recall, but the unanticipated surges of associated memories orbiting like a hungry galaxy; the taste which we believe to be reaching out to seize us from the mists of our history. It is more about *why* we remember it, or want to remember it, or of what world is the taste a whispered evocation.

Consequently, I am too much of a cynic to say, "I will remember how that tasted for the rest of my life," but if I was seized by such romanticist self-deception (it is Autumn after all), this is probably what I'd come up with:

1. **The Best Piece of Pizza I've Ever Had** was in Rome, just on the other side of some or other bridge; it had just stopped raining and suddenly the whole rotten city was glowing like all the ancient stone was sloughing off the accumulated light and warmth of so many centuries and I was just fit to vomit in defiance of its insidious perfection. The pizza was out of a little shop that sold mostly oils and dried pasta and the like. The pizza was thin, topped with buffalo mozzarella, fresh basil, green tomatoes, and olive oil in sufficient quantity and quality as to be undeniably a topping. It was so far from almost everything we have come to associate with pizza in North America, and yet it was not irreducibly a different thing. It was so fresh and vibrant, it was as if one was reaching back into the past of pizza, beneath a hundred-year-old patina of grease and burnt cheese, and tasting something pure and true[1]. I don't think the goddamn thing was even cooked, besides the crust, obviously. I told someone recently that I ate a piece of pizza in Rome that fundamentally altered my life, and I don't think they believed me. I suppose you had to be there.

---

1 I am never comfortable with this sort of fetishizing of some glorious untainted past; rhetoric of purity and authenticity is a treacherous thing that I always feel is leaving the door open for some race war or another, but in terms of the immediate associations I had with this pizza, I have to be honest. At the same time, I also don't begrudge North American pizza in its many permutations, I prefer to just see them as historically and culturally specific variations, some of which are bad, some of which are goddamn delicious.

2. **The First Time I Tasted Sichuan Pepper** was in Halifax, some return-home ago, in a clean, fresh little restaurant called Hungry Chili, which the Google Street View reveals to me is still in existence, but is from the outside at least, dirty as a dog's hat. I used to talk about it a lot, because golly, it was sincerely eye-opening and that dish of raw ginger and Sichuan peppercorn-heaped tofu singlehandedly inspired my beginning to take seriously the regional specificity of Chinese cuisine and my (presumably) tiresome and (definitely) ill-informed snobbishness about pan-Chinese (to say nothing of pan-Asian) restaurants. You really can't imagine the difference between a legitimately Sichuan restaurant and the fare from one of the Chinese grab-bag establishments one usually encounters. I could still further make the historically rigourless claim that this experience, by way of exciting a keener historical and geographical interest in food, was the first step in my starting to write about food at all. You're throwing your hands heavenward in gratitude, I'm sure.

I mean, it probably wasn't, but I'd probably believe it if I said it. Especially if I was like "Come on, man, *probably*."

3. Less for the taste, and more for the texture, temperature, and the "holy crap" nostalgic surround of **Eating Chocolate Ice Cream With A Fork**. Specifically Olympia brand, and specifically a two-litre tub, standing over the open deep freeze, because this is what my brother and I always did growing up. Somehow I think he got it in his head that a fork was ideally suited to digging out bits of ice cream and then disguising the evidence of having done so in a manner superior to a spoon. Admittedly, the spoon is with rare exception an obtuse and boorish utensil, and left such

identifiably spoon-like traces in the ice cream that our parents would be sure to detect our illicit excess ice cream consumption. That they were not imbeciles and could clearly a) discern that there was, like, half a litre of ice cream missing, and b) make the connection between said missing ice cream and the FORK MARKS everywhere did not seem to shake our faith in this method, which I of course adopted because he was my older brother and I did everything he did in order to become cooler (i.e. wear a trench coat, listen to The Cure, read comic books, nurture a thinly-veiled sense of superiority, look down one's nose at those who dressed up as non-scary/evil things for Hallowe'en, etc.).

This stark mental impression of the cold silkiness of the ice cream between the unyielding and still colder tines of the fork, the sweetness contrasted against the horrible metallic bite of old silverware, is one for which I will be forever in my brother's debt (for that and the "barbarian handshake"). Thanks, bro.

Engouement

Engouement, *noun* unreasoning fondness. Or, an excessive or irrational liking for something.

From the French, obviously, and I think rarely used in English, but what is interesting is the double meaning in French: both the above *"sentiments favourables et excessifs que l'on conçoit sans grande raison pour quelqu'un ou quelque chose,"* and the more literal meaning of "an obstruction in the throat."

It is curious, the idiomatic drift that relates having something stuck in your throat to an irrational fondness for a thing, but I think there exists an underlying resonance. What does it mean to qualify a preference or desire as both irrational and excessive? Can this speak to a liking that is distinguishable from taste (taste as sense, not as predilection) itself? In the case of food, could one have an *engouement* for a food the taste of which one does not actually enjoy? Is this wherein the irrationality lies?

Considered another way, do I have an *engouement* for chips? They are admittedly delicious, but my habit of eating way too many and the inevitable sickness and self-loathing that follow should, thinking rationally, steer me away from their consumption. Still, I persist.

Or could it be said of an *inappropriate* reason for liking something? Where one likes an aspect of something that does not ultimately serve as sufficient grounds for that liking (according to, you know, Them). I unfortunately can't think of a good culinary illustration of this at the moment, what comes more readily to mind is liking a person for some trivial or incidental reason.

But I guess we say this sort of thing all the time, "I like _____ way too much, considering they're not actually that good," etc.

I'd like to think that liking something out of spite figures into this conversation somehow. It brings to mind the skepticism of the aging aunt from MFK Fisher's "Social Status of a Vegetable" ("Surely you don't believe that I think your eating [cabbage] is anything more than a pose?")[1], and how irrationality plays (at least!) a dual function in our cultural register, re: food. It underlies the suspicion that occasionally meets foodies (although if you self-identify as such, you probably deserve it) and the gourmandizing set, and is mobilized in the form of a critique that ultimately calls into question their sincerity. As if it is not quite believable, not quite reasonable, that food per se, or foods in particular, could really merit such gross and fawning devotion. A veritable *culture of engouement* has 'food culture' become, in this evaluation. At the same time, it is a similar irrationality that lights from below our justifications for our weakness for junk food: "I really shouldn't like this, I know I shouldn't be eating this," etc. But try as we may (or may not), the fondness obstinately refuses to be Heimliched, and we develop a kindly affection for the obstruction.

---

1 See *"Brassica Uber Alles*, Part 1: Chouette First, Ask Questions Later?"

Of Black Mischief and Wastrelry

Homebrewing is a delicate art, or so they tell me. For whatever truth such a statement contains (and there is some, certainly), I believe that it is more often used to justify or soften a poor showing, or alternatively as a means to slyly play up the magnitude of one's own success. I have long been of the mind that if one is considering getting into the business (i.e. pleasure) of homebrewing, it stands to reason that beer is the way to go, for two reasons. The first is that it saves one the difficulties of selecting, buying, and pressing the grapes (because if you're going to do it, do it right, right?), and since so many of the particularities of any given wine depend on grape variety, region, and the like, that's a significant part of the craft process you are cutting out from the get-go. I suppose the same can be argued for beer, in that it is unlikely that one will be growing and malting one's own grain, or even one's own hops, and so it is perhaps on the second reason that my argument (ah, let's just call it a considered opinion) hinges: you have probably had more good homebrew than you have homemade wine, and if you haven't, you are either unusually fortunate or you need only to increase your n and this assertion will be borne out. Not to say that good homemade wine is a total anomaly, it just strikes me that it is easy to spend nine dollars on a bottle of wine (in Québec at least, probably still easier in much of the U.S.) that will be superior to what you will manage to produce even after a couple of years of practice. In contrast, while there is certainly room for disaster in beer making, there is more opportunity to stumble oafishly into a truly delicious brew, on par with the six- or seven-dollar pints one finds at the local microbrewery. Which is to say that I am inclined to believe that it suffers fools with an arbitrary alacrity that wine-making does not.

The first time that I tried to make beer, admittedly more as an assistant than an equal partner, we pretty much fucked up each and every step in some way, all the way through the process. I shan't get into details, but there was much over-boiling, confusion of hops, mistaking of instruments for other kinds of instruments, frantic phone calls, and late night scurryings-about, becoming increasingly cavalier as the night went on, disregarding such trivialities as precise measurements or cleanliness.

As it turned out, the product of all this haphazardness was a delicious espresso-chocolate stout (I have a problem with the word "mocha," okay? It just feels bad on the tongue, you know? Mocha? It makes me think about white people talking about jazz and sex in the same sentence. Ew, no.), all the more delicious after we gave it a good couple extra months of mellowing, aging, integration time. The downside was that whenever you opened a bottle it FUCKING EXPLODED EVERYWHERE (rugs, faces, beware), reducing our 500mL repurposed[1] Grolsch swing-tops to a flattish cup-and-a-quarter, if that. The first one even blew the *breugel* right off the bottle, such was the force of the frothy, geysering mon-

---

1 It may seem like I have succumbed to the allure of buzzwordery and am misusing the word "repurposed," but my argument is that Grolsch, being a lager, which I consistently dislike, is a sufficiently different beast from our dirty, confused, existentially angry stout that the use is justified. It is a hyperbolic gesture. Take that, Grolsch, or, alternatively, sponsor me. I'll learn to love you.

strosity. The beer was consequently christened Ratwagon for its unique self-ratwagoning[2] quality.

It was this beer, this happy accident of fortune, that led to the cementing of one, and by extension, the generation of another, of a couple of the fondest mixed drinks in my repertoire: the Noonday Reviver and the Black Mischief.

Kingsley Amis, in *Everyday Drinking* describes the Noon-day Reviver as a beer cocktail designed by Evelyn Waugh (whom I am generally all over, especially having acquired as particularly well-thought-out Christmas gifts both *The Selected Letters of...* and his "first"[3] autobiography *A Little Learning*, the end of which I have yet to tire of describing to half-bored party acquaintances), consisting of Guinness, gin, and ginger beer: "I cannot vouch for the authenticity of the attribution, which I heard in talk, but the mixture will certainly revive you, or something. I should think two doses is the limit." I attempted to reproduce this myself,

---

2 *ratwagon, noun 1.* A philosophical analogy describing human existence in terms of riding in a wagon mounted on or in a giant space rat that is both blind and insane, tearing through the cosmos blindly and insanely. Existential options limited to being Within the Ratwagon, or Without the Ratwagon, which unfortunately is The Void. **2.** A blind insane rat with a wagon in its back and wheels in lieu of hind legs.
verb The act whereby one seizes another person in a headlock, then runs around pouring beer on their head.
interjection (*RATWAGON!!!*) coll. – Exclaimed while in the process of ratwagoning someone.
3 *A Little Learning* was intended, as the subtitle states, to be *The First Volume of an Autobiography*, and covers only his childhood up until the end of Waugh's education/career in education; effectively up to just prior his writing career. The book ends with him, a malcontent schoolmaster and a rejected, dejected author, swimming out into the water with the intention to commit suicide, getting stung by a bunch of jellyfish and being like "ah, hell," then turning back, to become goddamn Evelyn friggin' Waugh. Two years after publication of *The First Volume* he died, leaving subsequent memoirs unwritten.

one time (not at noonday, mind you, but after dark) and was fabulously unsuccessful. I attribute this to using too sweet a brand of ginger beer and some manner of crossedness of stars, for which I cannot be held responsible. Not to be deterred, however, we tried it again with our homebrew, a better ginger beer, and a more confident measure of gin, and lo and behold it is quite a formidable and, dare I say it, *moreish* drink.

The Noonday Reviver has since come to serve as the foundation (conceptual and genealogical) for another drink, although for the precise conditions of the emergence of this latter I cannot fully account. Perhaps I was inspired by someone in particular? Just as likely it was a matter of convenience, of adaptation, of associative innovation, or perhaps merely of taste. What developed was a similar drink which substituted for the ginger beer a shot of straight espresso, and what one loses in gingeriness one gains in bitterness. In fact, much to my surprise, the result is something that still tastes more or less like a complex and challenging artisanal stout than it does a horrifying and wrongheaded mishmash of ingredients, which is often the attitude I encounter in response to my description of the Noonday Reviver. I think the strength of this substitution is that coffee, as evidenced by the prevalence of espresso stouts, is a natural complement to dark beers, whereas ginger beer, while not ill-suited per se, is potentially a more jarring addition to the intense panoply of flavours mingled already in the gin. The constitution thus varied, it fell to us to devise a new name for the drink, and in deference to its origins, we thought what more appropriate gesture than to plumb the Waugh bibliography for ideas. As if it were all foreordained, we settled superficially and inevitably upon *Black Mischief* (I mean, can you blame us?), a satirical novel about an English-educated emperor of a fictional African country's ill-fated attempts to modernize his backward and corrupt nation. The drink of course owes nothing to the plot of the book (which I have not actually read), but the title resonates satisfyingly with both its appearance and the type of conduct that is likely to result from such a combination of ingredients. The addition of coffee implies, if not guarantees, some mischief (the way Sparks implies, without guaranteeing, broken plate glass and an attempt to dig a tunnel under the freeway). So the name fits, even if Waugh himself might be unlikely to approve. I gather he was a pretty disapproving type all around, so I shan't get hung up on it. And Amazon.ca assures me that "This novel is not racist," which is good because I too am not racist.

And so, by way of recipe:

Evelyn Waugh's "Noonday Reviver"
(via Kingsley Amis)
1 hefty shot gin
1 (1/2 pint) bottle Guinness
ginger beer

Pour gin and Guinness into a pint glass, fill to top with ginger beer.

"Black Mischief" (via my own extensive, presumably scientific experimentation)
1 shot gin
1 shot espresso
Fill to taste with stout.

Should you order this in a bar, I suggest you spare yourself the embarrassment (and likely contempt of the bartender) by keeping the name to yourself and just ask for a pint of stout (we in Montréal are lucky enough to have the St-Ambroise Oatmeal Stout as a widely available option), a short espresso and a shot of gin. Unfortunately, this is likely to run you between eleven and thirteen dollars altogether, but I imagine if you're ordering it you've got a good reason. Drink the stout down slightly, pour in the gin, followed by the espresso, be prepared for grudging accolades, confusion, borderline disgust, or in the best case, adulation, even conversion.

Prozit.

We Return, Like Dogs, to Our Vomit...
(Only to Find it has Staled in the Meantime)

Six songs, all currently my favourite, having to do at least associatively with alcohol.

1. **Harry Belafonte – "Will His Love Be Like His Rum?"** Yes it will! Yes it will! Which is to say, intoxicating all night long. Mostly about marital bliss, this song is a toast to a happy couple with a happy future, or at least to an experience that is both invigorating and regrettable.

2. **Nina Simone – "Lilac Wine"** All sorts of people seem to know the Jeff Buckley version better, but Nina Simone kills it. Also associating love and drunkenness, but in this case it is a particular love, a particular liquor, a particular drunk and is particularly, world-sunderingly touching.

> *When I think more than I want to think*
> *do things I would never do*
> *I drink more than I want to drink,*
> *because it brings me back you...*
>
> *Lilac wine, is sweet and heady, like my love.*
> *Lilac wine, I feel unsteady, like my love.*
> *Listen to me... why is everything so hazy?*

I have this disproportionately fervent desire to try lilac wine sometime, assuming it will be thick and slow and altogether too sweet, presumably smelling of lilacs, and the type of thing that can only end honourably in reeling oblivion.

3. Stick McGhee – "Drinkin' Wine Spo-Dee-O-Dee" Usually attributed to and more famously known as by Jerry Lee Lewis, I much prefer this version, which you can find on the Atlantic Records Rhythm & Blues Collection, Volume 1 (1947-1952). It's less rip-roarin', but I find the leisurely pace resonates better with the usual experience of copious wine consumption.

In terms of songs such as this wherein good-natured drunken brawling figures prominently, I always think of Thin Lizzy's "The Boys Are Back In Town," I guess just for it evoking the onset of summer and getting riled up (*"Drink will flow and blood will spill, and if the boys wanna fight you'd better let 'em"*[1]); although I wouldn't say it's sufficiently booze-centric for me to include it on this list. "Having A Good Time," on the other hand—one of my all-time favourite drink-related, or in this case, drink-fueled songs—easily qualifies. It opens: *"Me and my buddies, we're gonna get drunk, we're gonna go out on the town. We'll be checking it out, slipping it in, and stepping out of line,"* and for the last two minutes of the song, Phil Lynott's lyrics sound like he is legitimately drunk, frozen forever in time in the artificial inebriate spontaneity of the recording. NB: also an excellent getting-ready-to-leave-the-house-pre-drinking (that being drinking-before-drinking, not doing-something-else-before-drinking) sort of song.

---

1 I have never in my life been in a non-amicable fight, brawl, or beatdown, and have not been beaten up in a good ten or fifteen years. I have much to say, however, for the merit of a friendly round of fisticuffs. I think it is in this spirit that Lynott writes of it, evoking the good-natured, ritualized, and consensual brutality of a sort of romantic masculinity that I have grown increasingly susceptible to/affectionate toward in the twilight of my youth.

4. The Techniques – **"Drink More Wine"** I can't seem to find the full lyrics anywhere online, and can't make out half of them myself, but it's a great little rocksteady jam by The Techniques, I believe during their period fronted by Slim Smith. The chorus is something to the effect of *"you must drink a lot of wine, and you will get well cool."* (Maybe?)

5. Paul McCartney – **"Monkberry Moon Delight"** When I was in grade eleven my best friend invented this drink at a party that he called "Mountain Moon Juice." It consisted, if I remember correctly, of Mountain Dew, vanilla ice cream, moonshine whiskey, orange juice, and blue food colouring, all blended to a uniform slurry. There may have been other ingredients, but I don't recall what. I do recall him drinking half of it, vomiting some green shit onto himself, partially disrobing, and then continuing to rage, shirtless, blender in hand (for that was the only suitable vessel out of which to drink Mountain Moon Juice), against the dying of the light; until, as expected, the light died and he passed out on the stairs. I may have some of the sequence wrong there. Maybe he lost his shirt, or vomited on it, borrowed my shirt, vomited on that, then went shirtless. I feel like my shirt got involved somehow. It is important to the charm of the story to know that he was not some rampaging high school jock, but very identifiably a pale, skinny, teen of the "hipster doofus" persuasion.

It's hard to tell what this nonsensical post-Beatles jibber-jabber is actually about, but when you listen to it, it sort of sounds like Mountain Moon Juice. Not the words, but the spirit thereof. It also sounds like that time the same best friend and myself took four hits of acid and stumbled into a bar to encounter a seven-person folk-rock band in matching tunics performing this very song. Things went downhill from there, I can tell you.

6. **Louis Jordan – "Boogie Woogie Blue Plate"** Not about alcohol so much, but a song about food that has caught my ear of late is Louis Jordan's "Boogie Woogie Blue Plate" (1947). Most noteworthy because it starts out by giving you the sense that it is not actually about food:

> *There's a gal at the local beanery,*
> *She's a pretty hunk of scenery*
> *She can make a chocolate soda go shhhhhh*
> *You should come out and dig it when*
> *she's working at the spigot...*

And then turns out, over the course of the next five verses, to actually be about food. Get your mind out of the gutter, for once.

Can Ye Never Go Home?

"_____ *is my bread and butter.*" So visceral is my reaction to the taste of (warm, probably white) bread and butter, to even the thought of it, that something goes awry whenever I try to invoke that simple commonplace. The thing is in excess of the idiom; the analogy breaks down as whatever it is that I am trying to talk about is intruded upon by the chain of associations brought about by that damn bread and that damn butter.

Pat's Rose & Grey was the only restaurant I can remember my parents taking me to as a child. There must have been others, although probably not many, my parents being as they were very DIY, nigh-hippy types[1]. They had complimentary breadsticks and breadsticks were somehow my favourite food. I always wanted to go to Pat's and I only ever wanted their breadsticks. I don't recall the rest of the food, any particular events or occasions, their decor (perhaps it was dim?)—only breadsticks. And butter. Not the hard crumbly breadsticks, but warm, soft miniature loaves, nestled in my brainstem amidst associations of comfort and total gustatory absorption[2].

Pat's Rose & Grey became the Island Rock Cafe, in whose

---

1 There was also King's Palace, which I remember as a murk of fake waterfalls,
all-you-can-eat egg rolls, jello and sweet & sour spare ribs, but this was later in life.
2 See also "When There's No One To Blame But Yourself."

kitchen I got my first job (dishpig, hired on the spot, worked for nine and a half hours straight. There was a maggot episode that I'd rather not get into), and outside of which I remember standing in the rain, fourteen years old, listening rapt to my father's band covering "Moondance", before shuffling off to eat Fritos in the parkade, alone (Fritos were magic, somehow. A solitary indulgence in an era of self-imposed (economic) leanness, improbably suited to rallying my spirits in my middle adolescence. Another taste which still takes me back. I like salt. A lot.).

—

The Island Rock Cafe became Brennan's, in whose kitchen I worked prep for the first time, was disburdened of my distrust of mushrooms by a short, mild-tempered cook's roasting of their stems with garlic, olive oil, and lemon juice. Also where I first learned the expression "jailbait", and in whose walk-in cooler, I first heard and identified with Morrissey's *"I was looking for a job and then I found a job, and heaven knows I'm miserable now."*

—

Potent associations with the space dwindle in the intervening years, and when I was last home I heard that it had been closed and sold again, and the new owners are ripping out all the old interior—the marble bar, wrought iron, and Venetian arcade affectations—all kicked to the curb. Rumours of an impending transformation into a dance bar for aging single ladies. I can't say I'll miss it, really, but I can imagine a time in the distant future when I walk by it and am all like "huh."

They also all had baked spaghetti. I remember liking that a lot.

Paneity

Paneity, *noun* the quality or state of being bread.

I am exactly the type of asshole who delights in knowing a word like paneity, but am also, thankfully, the type who has the good sense never to use it. The exceptions being here, now; and this weekend while playing Scrabble when I was like one goddamn letter away from knocking everyone's socks off with my lexicographical prowess.

And I think the word is special that way, like a little talisman that you hold close to your heart and take out only from time to time to look at and appreciate, because I do love the way it sounds and what it conjures up. There's something in the "ei" that to me evokes the tenderness and elasticity of the glutinous.

Because of this specialness, it seems vulgar and annoying when someone actually uses the word, outside of the most extenuating of circumstances.

This is in part because I think the word *breadiness* does just fine for the purpose. I do not resent that an obscure "proper" word exists, but I think to use it in common parlance is unnecessarily portentous, if not downright pretentious.

Of further interest (assuming the presence of initial interest) there is also a theological dimension to the word. Within discussions of transubstantiation, the process whereby the bread and wine of the Eucharist *become* the body and blood of Christ, paneity refers to the state of being merely bread. How about that, hey?

When in Doubt, Put Some Gravy on It

Embarking on the preliminary research for what I hoped might stand as the ultimate paean to gravy, I find myself mired (pleasantly so) in the surprisingly interesting historical and chemical miscellany of starch.

There are all sorts of interesting tidbits in the chapter "Sauces Thickened With Flour and Starch" of Harold McGee's *On Food and Cooking*, tidbits which have substantially confounded my embarrassingly dismissive prior opinion of the starches.

In my head, "starch" previously conjured up cornstarch alone (a "cheap," as in morally bankrupt, thickener), and hazy chemistry class memories of bananas horribly blackened by—what? Lithium? Iodine? Leafing through the chapter, however, I can only be embarrassed by my prior dismissiveness. Indeed , when I read that starch is "the molecule in which most plants store the energy they generate from photosynthesis," I may have shouted aloud something like "Man, starches are actually really cool!" And by the end of the lengthy description of the process of its acquisition by the ancient Romans, involving multiple grindings of flour, soakings in water, harnessings of the power of mighty bacteria to digest the cell walls and proteins of the grain, and finally drying in the sun in a veritable Planeteersian team effort (I guess the bacteria is heart?), I was sold! By sold, I mean I had overcome my previous prejudice against the idea of starch-thickened sauces, although like a fuck, I will probably stick to flour.

Anyway, gravy is a wonderful thing. An ongoing point of contention in the warehouse where I work is my tendency, as a once-vegan, to unproblematically refer to vegan bastardizations of specific dishes by their 'original' names, *sans* vegan prefix, by which my coworkers are invariably scandalized (their mock confusion begins to wear on me). An obvious example would be any time I talk about fake meat, eschewing out of laziness the qualifiers "mock," "soy," "gluten," *etc*:

Me: "Man, I made this delicious meatball sub the other night with sweet potato fries in it. You know, you wouldn't think the sweet potato would work so much, what with the sweetness and the marinara sauce, but it was actually pretty epic."

Skeptical Coworker: "Wait, I thought you didn't eat meat?"

Me: "I don't. Vegan meatballs."

Skeptical Coworker: "That is not a meatball."

Me: "Whatever, it is more or less a meatball. It serves the same basic function as a meatball, i.e. being meaty, being ball-shaped, being totally excessive when put in a sandwich, right?"

Skeptical Coworker: "Yeah, *not* a meatball."

Me: "Yeah, *anyway,* please allow me to continue telling you about this epic sandwich already, this *vegetarian meatball sandwich*, or do you suddenly have something better to do, like your job?"

Skeptical Coworker: "Why not just call it a soy ball?"

Me: "Because it is not merely a soy ball, it is a combination of gluten and soy, and no one is going to eat a 'gluten soy ball'."

Skeptical Coworker: "Well no one *should* eat a gluten

soy ball."

Me: "Shit, have you seen fifty-two copies of *Digital Fortress*?"

Likewise, anytime I refer to cream sauces, *béchamel*, etc., I get called out for my refusal to use either milk or cream (which I acknowledge as glaringly arbitrary, given my prodigious cheese consumption). These tiffs occasionally escalate into accusations that I must secretly abominate the French (or at least the venerable institution of their cuisine), using *soy milk* as I do, and of course, how can I even expect anything to turn out right, making such an egregious sub-stitution?[1] A criticism to which to a certain extent I concede, because yes, cream and soy milk are chemically not of the same realm; just as one cannot rely upon margarine to behave as butter in any but the most superficial applica-tions, such as making toast more delicious and less dry. Try to serve anyone anything in a *margarine blanc* sauce and you'll get only the aggravated assault you deserve.

However, to all the unilateral butter supremacists who refuse to see margarine as anything but a hopeless, irre-deemable, and pathetically ersatz pretender to the throne, I counter that *what margarine can do that butter never can is* to *make something taste like it is covered in margarine*. Which, look down your nose all you please, amounts to making something taste like it is covered in salty oil, and if you can't appreciate that you best step back, because brother, life is but an empty coffin, and you's being a touch too selective about how you fills it.

---

1 In my defense, Clotilde Dusoulier, genuine Frenchwoman and gastronome of *Chocolate & Zucchini* (www.chocolateandzucchini.com) fame has on her website endorsed the use of soy or almond milk substitutes in *béchamel*. Eat that.

But before I stray too far afield, let us get back to gravy.

In all fairness to The Bastards (and/or my coworkers), gravy really is a sauce made from the juices and detritus of cooked meats, thickened with starch or flour—each recipe or manifestation defined in part by its last-minute concoction. In fact, this economy of ingredients and slapdash constitution is not only part of its charm but part of its distinction from other sauces—a long-cooked French brown sauce for example—part of its identity *qua gravy*, arguably.

On the topic of "arguably," in contrast to many vegan/vegetarian variations on traditionally meaty foodstuffs, vegetarian gravy occupies the rare position of actually already having a pre-existing non-meat-specific appellation. Mock chicken is *mock* chicken because I guess you could call it a gluten wad or whatever (which a lot of Asian packaging already does, god love their no-nonsense ESL labelling), but mushroom gravy and peppercorn gravy and miso gravy really needn't be called gravy per se, because they are not meat-based and not even really fat-based and there are already all sorts of sauces to which they bear a keener resemblance.

So why not *sauce*? Miso sauce, peppercorn sauce, mushroom sauce?

Very simply: *gravy rules*.

Put in other words, this is sort of the same as the answer to "why mock chicken and not gluten wad?" We are attracted to the familiar, it evokes something we as vegetarians miss or conjures up positive associations, blah blah blah... But it is also different, because (duh) gravy rules and you know it does. It's not just a sauce, it's *gravy*, and yeah, we all know that every family's gravy is different, but we also know that gravy means rich and it means savoury and it means salty and probably brown, and *still more* that the appetite of our reptilian brain has been aroused and the better angels of our nature are not merely about to be put to sleep, but suffocated with our mashed potatoes, dinner pies, and biscuits, as our previous desire to Eat Some Food is subsumed into our desire to Impenitently Use Food As A Medium For Gravy. By this savoury deluge, previous centerpieces of the meal are reduced to thin (albeit delicious in their own right) pretext; gravy begins as a condiment and ends as a food. Gravy is a usurper, and this we know when we break bread with it, and that's what's *great*—and all this (expansive arm gesture), really, was intended as a vaguely interesting preamble to me talking about how I want you to eat more gravy, and how I want you, above all, not to be *afraid* of gravy. In summation:

Points on Approaching the Realness of Gravy

1. You can call it sauce if you want to, but you probably won't, because, in spite of the above quibbling, gravy *as an idea* is the *license that frees us from the constraints of the recipe*, which frees us from the fear of fucking up a sauce (which has honestly been worrying at my bloodied heels like feral dogs ever since I got it into my head that I should develop a "solid foundation in traditional French saucery," (I have not).), and allows us to really, well, Go Big Or Go Home, or to not if we don't feel like it. Gravy has the benefit of being very processual—it is so easy to work on a gravy for a while (this is the difference between gravy of the spirit (my gravy) and gravy of the letter (simple, meat n' flour gravy), the latter being quick, the former necessarily somewhat longer term), believe it's going well, add a few things, ruin it, then

with either careful attention or a couple of inspired creative flourishes (i.e. booze), catapult it into the right hand of grace! Gravy is thus *endlessly redeemable*, so long as one believes in gravy and believes in oneself (duh).

2. *Roux:* don't worry about it, it's easy. If not butter, then margarine. If not margarine, oil. Equal parts flour and fat, cooked to one of three degrees—moisture reduced, but flour still whitish; flour cooked to golden paste; flour cooked to brown (or supposedly red, hence *roux/rouge*), and then the slow integration of water, broth, soy milk, beer, wine (see below, and above), whatever.

3. Booze, dear friend. Wine, whiskey, beer, friggin' whatever. NB: if you're working with soy milk, beware of the acidity of the alcohol causing gnarly separation, but just mind your business, and shit'll work out.

4. Yeah, believe in yourself. Also believe in fresh *coarsely ground black pepper*. Possibly a mix of peppers.

5. Uhhhhhhhhh... I put it on everything?

When There's No One To
Blame But Yourself...

Blame a shapeless externality? Fate or The Fates? The Bastards (*non carborundum*)? An unfortunately perfect storm of Boredom, Weather, History and Fear?

Or, more tangibly (but only slightly more definite in shape) "The Island"?

It's difficult "coming home", when you're discomfitingly aware that you're going to be looking forward to "going (back) home" (where you live the rest of the time) in a week, and you're fairly certain that you only really have one Home at a time and in that case you'd probably prefer the one that occasions less dread.[1] Prince Edward Island is not a very exciting place, a grim reality of which Mike (a fellow islander) and I were quite aware when we lived there, and about which we had no illusions when we decided to go back and see our respective parents and family pets. (NB: the Tourism PEI website's featured Story "Island Seasons," which begins "Islanders enjoy four very distinct seasons..." and goes not much of anywhere.)

You find yourself drinking more, watching more television, wearing sunglasses at odd hours, vaguely scheming to sleep with people you would, frankly, normally avoid, and, evidently, going to East Side Mario's.

It was approximately 10:00am, and we were one warm-

---

1 If my parents are reading this, I mean of course "Home" as in "The Island," not their physical architectural home, nor the figurative or spiritual home constituted by their embrace/presence/etc...

Stella-for-breakfast each into what could have turned out to be a Good Day; not entirely sure where we had parked the car the previous night, nor what it was I had done to Mike's face ("What did you do to my face?! I have to see my *grandmother* today."), but it all seemed immaterial to me. Less so was the matter of *breakfast*.

In retrospect I should perhaps find it strange that there was no discussion of the fitness of East Side Mario's for such a purpose, but in our defense there was a hot sun beating mercilessly down upon us and the streets we walked, and the promise of inexhaustible Free Bread With Your Meal within (I don't know that this was advertised, but it certainly seemed to be something we knew).

This bread, might I say, was fantastic.

Really hit the spot. Little pat of butter and everything. Comes to your table on a little cutting board all warm and already impaled on a (steak?) knife. I can't recommend this sort of thing enough for a hangover, and at this point do not hesitate to say that we were soaring (by "this point," I mean having ordered and already on our third loaf of Free Bread), just on top of the world, our dim little world (the sunglasses again, remember). Willing to forgive our simply horrendous daiquiris, so full of magnanimity and benevolence and peace and bread and daiquiris we were.

Unfortunately, things took a bit of a turn.

I won't bore you with (nor am I in possession of) the specifics of our meal, but I had Caesar salad and asparagus linguini Alfredo. This is not something that exists on the menu proper, but the people at East Side Mario's are nothing if not accommodating, you see.

Then, fuck it, maybe another (awful) daiquiri and definitely a still worse Bellini, which Mike was under the (not mistaken, under ideal circumstances) impression was something like a champagne daiquiri, but apparently in the terrifying bizarro Italo-Americano-world that is East Side Mario's contains some manner of hard liquor and maybe poison? Some kind of poison? And some sort of laboratory-spawned (there was grave desecration and electricity involved, I'm sure of it) hyper-saccharine syrup that immediately causes brain damage and fuses the Positive Mental Attitude morning drunk (edge taken off, pleasantly squared away, etc.) with its villainous shadow The Fear (o, hateful Gemini!). It was regrettable and I do not recommend it.

Mike had, among other things edible that I cannot recall, a message from the kitchen consisting solely of "HELLO FROM THE RED DRAGON," delivered not even by our own waiter, but by some other waitfellow, so accommodating are these people. Our first thought, naturally, was *"Our disguises!"*

Here it may be necessary to explain that, external to any considerations of looking sharp, living smart, the accursed sun, or Coping With Life; our shiny shoes, previously clean(er) dress shirts and inconspicuous black Ray-Bans were also intended to serve as an impenetrable blind so that no unsavoury characters out of our pasts, however peripheral, could recognize and apprehend us, forcing us to embark down an irreversible path of elaborate misrepresentation and outright fabulation regarding our Success At Life Thus Far (have I mentioned that this summer was our ten-year high school reunion and we weren't even invited, assuming that there was something to be invited to?). You can imagine how well this worked, I'm sure.

Anyway, at the time we were both dumb and confounded

that someone had managed to see through our cunning dissemblance and recognize us *from so far away as the interior of the kitchen*, no less! What could this foretell?

Things are pretty hazy and characterized by much mewling and gnashing of teeth and maligning whatever forces external to us had brought such gastronomical and psychological misfortune down upon us, and the whole thing sort of resolved itself by us deciding to sleep the rest of the afternoon away in the car, counting on our natty dress, fine automobile, and the inability of others to smell us to protect us from molestation by the authorities ("Clearly, we are but two nonspecifically successful and well-adjusted business types taking but a power nap after lunch, before returning to whatever loosely scheduled and cutting edge industry it is that employs us!").

In closing, I say go to East Side Mario's, probably. I mean, if you're going to go, you're going to go—the Statue of Liberty holds aloft a tomato, for god's sake—and if that doesn't tell you what you're getting into, then god help you. The food was passable, unterrible—all things considered—the drinks were not, and I probably spent something like thirty dollars by the last. I think the pasta might have even been okay. But they didn't make us take off our sunglasses, and there was a pleasing surfeit of candles in those nice wicker-wrapped bulbous wine bottles one associates with Italys and Little Italys the world over.

Anyway, I blame the island. And the cursed sea that cradles it.

Food as Destroyer

So I left her with figs stuffed in my trouser pockets and in my jacket, figs in both of my outstretched hands, and figs in my mouth. I couldn't stop eating them and was forced to get rid of the mass of plump fruits as quickly as possible. But that could not be described as eating; it was more like a bath, so powerful was the smell of resin that penetrated all my belongings, clung to my hands and impregnated the air through which I carried my burden. And then, after satiety and revulsion—the final bends in the path— had been surmounted, came the ultimate mountain peak of taste. A vista over an unsuspected landscape of the palate spread out before my eyes—an insipid, undifferentiated, greenish flood of greed that could distinguish nothing but the stringy, fibrous waves of the flesh of the open fruit, the utter transformation of enjoyment into habit, of habit into vice. A hatred of those figs welled up inside me; I was desperate to finish them, to liberate myself, to rid myself of all this overripe, bursting fruit. I ate to destroy it. Biting had rediscovered its most ancient purpose.

– "Fresh Figs," Walter Benjamin (May, 1930)

Benjamin's "I ate to destroy it" has that peculiar density of resonance such that once one reads it, it continues to echo not only forward, throughout the rest of one's days, but backward into one's past, to put it clumsily. It is as if one had heard it long ago, and it had been echoing, unidentified, all along, up until the moment when suddenly years of vague impressions and indistinct syllables resolved themselves into a simple phrase and one was able to say, "Oh, this is what I was hearing all along." I am tempted to make a further analogy of something reverberating on a visceral level finally being rendered intelligible in thoughts and words, but then it might sound like I was capable of appreciating poetry, and I can't risk that. Suffice to say, "I ate to destroy it" speaks to a sort of savage rearticulation of one's relationship to a food, beyond hunger, beyond appetite, beyond a pleasure that can easily be called gastronomic.

For Benjamin, there is a purity (dangerous, like all purities) in this, but in "Fresh Figs" he stops just short of addressing the dark underside of Eating To Destroy, that is, its inversion. There is a specter that haunts this act, drives and derides it, that is *Food As Destroyer*.

Crapulence possesses me regularly, both conceptually and literally. Which is to say that I have spent a lot of time thinking about eating, excess, shame, sickness and revulsion, as well as personally being sick from over-consumption. It should be obvious how sickness from excessive eating relates to the notion of "food as destroyer," although they are not reducible one to the other. This goes beyond being merely seduced by a food into overeating; rather it is both more and less. In attempting to explain Food As Destroyer, it occurs to me that it is perhaps best approached from the side, rather than head-on. And so it is not making oneself sick from (over) eating that concerns me here, but rather *what one eats when one is (already) sick*. In my own case there exists a delicate and fraught relationship between *comfort food* and thanatotic (see "as destroyer") food.

We all have comfort food, at least those of us for whom the idea of "having a relationship to food" is intelligible.[1] By comfort food, I mean that to which we turn at times of physical or emotional duress, food that is conventionally less challenging or inspiring than it is soothing, predictable. This is food that is "always there when you need it," as it were. I should like to specify that while I am drawing on the cultural currency of the notion of "comfort food," I am not totally comfortable with the manner in which it has become partly fixed in the landscape of Western food culture. That "Ten Best Comfort Foods" can be cried from the cover of a magazine indicates a subtle misapprehension, and dare I say (because I don't often), a co-option of comfort food. In principle, comfort food can be any food one turns to for solace, but it is often tied to one's upbringing, and by association, the simple, unassuming fare of the "family recipe." This is all well and good, but has become something of a trope, and I fear is beginning to take on a categorical quality. I am skeptical of recipes that stake their claim to comfort *a priori*, framing themselves as classic, "just like mom used to make," American standards, thus constituting a hegemonic register (or recipe book) of "Comfort Food" that may have little to do with the idiosyncratic and intensely personal items that make up comfort food when it is thought descriptively rather than prescriptively.

---

1 It is on faith alone that I accept that there exist those people who move through the world indifferent to what they put in their bodies, so long as it meets their basic survival need. Such characters, with their emotionless or at least emotionally uncomplicated engagements with food, will remain forever slightly opaque to me, like people who don't read books or listen to music ("I just listen to whatever's playing on the radio"), and I suppose the notion of "comfort food" seems to them similarly incomprehensible.

This is not a big deal. I'm not angry at "comfort food." I like, you know, cheesecake or whatever. But when comfort food becomes unmoored from biography, we have some bad shit going down. "Comfort food," regardless, is a fairly ambiguous category. Do we seek different manners of comfort for different types of ailments; emotional, physiological, spiritual? How are they distinct from or overlapping with the food we eat when we are sick in order to (hopefully) become less sick?

For example, when I am sick and want to get better but still eat something delicious, I usually turn to brown rice and steamed kale, probably with a very ginger-, garlic-, and nutritional yeast-heavy miso-tahineh sauce. Easy to digest, got some greens in there, got other aggressively healthy shit in there, but it's still salty as hell, therefore good. But even though I thoroughly enjoy it, this is not a comfort food.

When it is specifically a *comfort food* I'm looking for while sick, I usually make a can of tomato soup with shit-tonnes of oregano and garlic and cayenne and olive oil, and several heavily-margarined slices of toast. This is where the real comfort comes in, along with the first stirrings of the death drive, oddly. Because you can't eat tomato soup without toast, right? Duh. This would be all well and good, but always I end up *continuously making toast* over the entire course of my consumption of the soup, usually resulting in me eating, oh, seven to ten pieces of toast, and probably a cup of margarine in total, and being so hideously gorged that my body has to divert all its energies into digesting the oily glue heap in my stomach instead of repairing/repelling whatever illness I should be battling.

Somewhere in the process of this meal (say, four toasts in?), I become faintly conscious that I am "eating to destroy"—not just the food, but *myself*.

This becomes more patently obvious in my tendency to eat chips and chocolate bars when I'm sick, in full cognizance of the fact that not only is it doing me no good, but that I am doing it in part to Do Me No Good, to, in fact, Do Me Ill.

See, I used to be sick a lot, and this really fostered an antagonistic Cartesian split in my life. It basically goes like this: I get sick, and then am all like "WTF, BODY? I treat you well with whole grains and some other healthy nonsense and this is how you go and do me? Well how do you like *this*?" as I stuff a fistful of chips into my mouth, "and THIS!" the next fistful of chips, and so on, until I have eaten an entire bag of Ruffles or whatever it is. And for a moment I feel a perverse sort of victory that is part sheer delight at having tasted delicious chips for such an extended period of time, part the guilty pleasure that comes with eating an entire bag of chips (not unlike the shameful self satisfaction of spending a month's rent on booze), and part mad Flagellant monk *triumph over the body* that says "Hey body, what's up? Bet you feel like shit, eh? Well, *how you like me now?!* Remember, I made you (untrue, admittedly) and I *can unmake you*, never forget that." As if you're teaching your stupid body some sort of lesson for being self-preserving enough to get sick. It's really insane, but that's how it goes.

What makes it all the more perverse (or all the less? I can't even tell anymore) is that there's a sort of liberating *jouissance* to this chip-eating paroxysm. I feel like I rarely more fully experience the potato chip—the salt just seems more alive on the tongue, and when one reaches (sooner than usual) the level of depravity of scarfing whole mouthfuls of chips at a time, there is a certain satisfaction in their jagged edges jabbing into and scraping the roof of the mouth, gums, tongue, inside lips, and it becomes a trial to even crunch through the haphazard formation, but a trial all the more worth undergoing for the reward of reducing it all to a pulpy, starchy, salty mass in the back of the mouth. At which point there is a moment of calm. The fire in the brain settles, serenely, like the storm of chips now reduced to a placid, masticated sea of potato purée; a chaos of angularity and imbrication into a sort of ordered formlessness. A collapsing of states.

No one who has never eaten a food to excess has ever really experienced it, or fully exposed himself to it. Unless you do this, you at best enjoy it, but never come to lust after it, or make the acquaintance of that diversion from the straight and narrow road of the appetite which leads to the primeval forest of greed. For in gluttony two things coincide: the boundlessness of desire and the uniformity of the food that sates it. Gourmandizing means above all else to devour one thing to the last crumb. There is no doubt that it enters more deeply into what you eat than mere enjoyment.
– Benjamin, 1930

Right?

Refrain, If At All Possible, From Calling It "Baba G"

While there is more than sufficient evidence available that I should not be listened to, let's be honest: if you buy store-bought baba ghanouj you're a sap. Because by and large you eat it and you're like, "Awesome, this tastes like mediocre over-lemony store-bought hummus that maybe some freakish eggplant man sat on or in or thought about eating, but it really doesn't taste like baba ghanouj, as if I know what that is anyway."

Which is why I for so long thought that despite loving eggplant, I didn't really care about baba ghanouj, because I was too lazy to roast a whole eggplant to make a dip (the same way I'm too lazy to pit like five-hundred olives to make a good tapenade) and just not-self-hating-enough to go buy it from a store. That is, until I had some really exceptional baba ghanouj from Marché Akhavan in NDG, which actually tasted like eggplant and tahineh and garlic and oil, and was real and good, and inspired me to rene-gotiate my relationship with this most venerable of dips. (Doesn't even the word "dip" seem denigrative and trivial-izing? I'm suspicious that the western hummus, tapenade , baba ghanouj, etc. = "dip" = party snack = "not real food" equation is partly responsible for our tacit acceptance of the poor treatment of the above by the packaged food industry. No pride.)

And now I act is if it's my place to say. Typical.

The trick, as I see it, is not being afraid of the weight

of the ingredients. And by this I mean not the physical weight, or even density, but the, how to say, burliness of the flavours involved. Take burliness as a variation on robust, robust being not quite the right word for these tastes, allowing burliness to do for flavour as robust does for paleo-anthropological physiology (as in, the distinguishing of the Neanderthals by their robust jawbone, suitable for grinding of hard seeds and grain). Bringing us, of course, to eggplant, garlic, and tahineh.

This, essentially, is baba ghanouj, along with olive oil, salt and lemon juice. The eggplant roasted, obviously. Beyond this one must proceed as they see fit. For my own part, I am inclined toward less lemon juice, more olive oil, and lots of tahineh, as I feel its bitter nuttiness (uh...seediness?) complements the smokiness of the roasted eggplant. The eggplant must be roasted whole if possible, by the way, and stuck here and there with a good thin sticker or perhaps boning knife. You'll know it's done when it has visibly expired-seeming to have given up its spongy ghost and resigned itself to its new existence as a brown, oily, smashed-octopus-looking mess-and sort of collapsed on itself. To further round out the body of the dish, I believe it is essential to roast the garlic as well-two bulbs to a good sized eggplant should do. Just toss it in the oven after the eggplant has had a few good minutes and you should be able to retrieve it at the same time, just at the point where the outermost cloves' surfaces are developing a sweet, deep brown caramelized layer beneath their skin. Do not shy away from the burned and blackened, where baba ghanouj is concerned! I'm telling ye, it is the key (one of several) to creating something you can be proud of, a dip that holds at its heart a mystery which resists even your best attempts (enticed by its deliciousness) at total assimilation into the body. Add a clove or so of finely minced raw garlic just to give it bite, the sharp top notes sounding with and against the mellow roundness of the roasted garlic.

Finally, and I will grant that this may not be essential to a good baba ghanouj, but I think a goodly blob of harissa does wonders. Its smoky spiciness complements the eggplant and garlic well, and the warm curious under-taste of coriander and caraway it imparts serves to magnify the aforementioned mystery that lurks at the heart of the dip. By this point (plus a little parsley) you should have arrived at a baba ghanouj which is rich and delicious and engaging. But no matter how much of it you eat (all of it, probably), you still feel as if something central has eluded you-as if you were attempting to eat your way to the core of a truth that confounds you by erecting walls beyond walls of delicious spicy eggplant muck so that eventually, inevitably you stall, defeated and slightly sickened, momentarily satisfied by eating fully to excess, but with spirits flagging, knowing that somehow you fell short of a worthwhile, if not indispensable revelation.

Perhaps it is merely that you seek a peace that is unattainable, because it is one based on the comfort of banality, whereas the baba ghanouj itself, constructed thusly of perhaps too many bold and resistant ingredients (harissa and tahineh come particularly to mind here, when speaking of tastes that force you to accommodate their own realities, instead of acquiescing to your own middling expectations) refuses to be wholly reconciled to the goals implicit in your act of eating; harbouring, at and even beyond the point of total consumption, shadowy motives all its own. And so, what now do I ask of baba ghanouj? Oh, only that it make demands of me that I cannot meet.

Also, my house is positively overrun with ants.

Gulchin

Gulchin, *noun* a little glutton.

I'd like to point out that this specifies not someone who is slightly gluttonous (sort of a contradiction in terms), but a glutton of diminutive stature, such as a child, dwarf, or I suppose, tiny voracious goblin of some description.

Probably derived, as with gulch, from the Middle English *gulchen*, meaning "to gush forth" or "to drink greedily" (see also: **gulchingly,** *adjective.* greedily, voraciously), in an interesting inversion. I think what happened here is that gulchen became gulch, "to gulp," and thus gulchin as a diminutive thereof.

Like how we get munchkin from *munchk*, meaning "a large annoying elf."

When "Nothing Special"
Is Distinctively, Arrestingly Special

In *Everyday Drinking* (2008), Kingsley Amis describes the Metaphysical Hangover, the often more detrimental to one's capacity for pleasure and self-worth sibling of the Physical Hangover—with which I'm sure we're all familiar:

> Perhaps Kafka's story *The Metamorphosis*, which starts with the hero waking up one morning and finding he has turned into a man-sized cockroach, is the best literary treatment of all. When that ineffable compound of depression, sadness (these two are not the same), anxiety, self-hatred, sense of failure, and fear for the future begins to steal over you, start telling yourself that what you have is a hangover. You are not sickening for anything, you have not suffered a minor brain lesion, you are not all that bad at your job, your family and friends are not leagued in a conspiracy of barely maintained silence about what a shit you are, you have not come at last to see life as it really is.

Within my circle we have come to refer to this complex simply as The Fear, and developed our own strategies for dealing with it (perhaps "dealing with" is less accurate than "suffering duly with approximately the dignity of a broke-dick dog"). Recognition, certainly, is of the essence, as is reconciliation. The latter to the reality that you cannot solve or cure The Fear, but at best mechanically and faithlessly administer palliatives. You must avoid the temptation to believe that there is Some Thing that you could eat that would make you feel slightly better. This heavily trodden path is one of steadily compounding dissatisfaction, and leads only to feeling still more bloated and self-sick. Although I can't quite explain the whys of it, I recommend listening to The Pixies or Depeche Mode (it just feels like they understand, somehow) while doing the washing up; for doing dishes, however unpleasant, is one of few activities that is sure to leave you better off than you were beforehand, and with The Fear one needs all the help one can get. Following this, tuck into a hearty mid-afternoon breakfast of spaghetti and pancakes and sit yourself down just shy of loathing-distance away from someone similarly beFeared to watch something inoffensive, like Star Trek or Futurama. So long as you can defend yourself from the poisonous temptation of self-reflection until the sun goes down, you'll probably be alright.

So goes the Metaphysical Hangover.

Today, however, is one of those lucky days when one wakes up with, or wanders into shortly after waking, the emotional inversion of such a soul-crushing consequence of Too Fine a Taste for the Excess of Things In Life—what I have dubbed the Sublime Hangover. In the grip of a Sublime Hangover you inexplicably feel good, still as if someone had poured a bottle of vodka all over your brain and the nerves in your teeth (as well they may have), but you are surfing, in lieu of sinking in, the void. Or perhaps better put, with a little less flash and hot-doggery, skiffing the void. It is as if one is got up in the metaphysical equivalent of deck shoes (no socks) and an open-at-the-neck cotton Polo just, you know, skiffin'. The light seems a little brighter, although

48

not oppressively or aggressively so; the withered outer veil of the flesh has been torn away, leaving you reveling in the beauty and serenity of the Real World like some wide-eyed and skinless gibbering abomination. Just so do I find myself, toddling, positive and alcohol-sodden, to and fro, up and down the same street for the better part of two hours (it's like I'd never been there in my life), until it occurs to me that I am not far off from the general area in which I had been told was located a little resto that serves up a quite satisfactory "chickpea shami" (sandwich). Undeterred by the lack of a name to go on, or anything more than the information that it is tiny, easy to miss, and occupies a barren stretch of *Avenue des Pins* wherein neither myself nor anyone I know had ever remarked a restaurant or really much of anything besides piles of uncollected garbage, I strike out in search, bolstered by the heady optimism of an only partially-functioning nervous system.

After some while furtively poking around, I walk through an unprepossessing doorway not unlike an ugly apartment building or commercial entrance to a bedroomware factory outlet (which in fact it is) and literally in the hallway leading in (it would be inaccurate and aggrandizing to call it a foyer), I discover a couple of stools and a little lunch counter. Behind the counter stands a man with dark hair, keen eyes, and a dusty olive complexion, whose name I'm given to understand is Nouri. Welcome to Chez Nouri.

I am hauntingly enamoured with this place already.

I sit on my stool and am suspended in the cottony silence peculiar to old, desiccated warehouses and office buildings—those that seem derelict before their time, that have perhaps outlived their relevance but nonetheless persist. Nouri has his little radio tuned to a classical station, whose soundtrack adds a gravity to his calm, deliberate movements as he navigates the narrow space he shares with only a fridge, a stove, a sink, and some cupboards. I had earlier consumed a triple-chocolate-orange cookie for breakfast with my coffee, and wonder whether it is the caffeine/sugar terror combining with my hangover's weakly lurching stomach that laces the serenity of the whole experience with an unsettling frisson of dislocation and uncertainty. Nouri heats the pita for my shami on a stove-top element and fills it with spiced chickpea mash (not hummus, something... burgery, or once fried, but still creamy and soft), tomatoes, lettuce, pickle, and tzatziki. It is simple and comforting, delicately spiced, and nothing special, but simultaneously *very, very special*.

I cannot help thinking that if I come back here often enough something important will happen. I will learn something, or I'll fall in love, or become embroiled in some manner of international intrigue. I will improbably by virtue of mistaken identity find myself pursued, racing through the streets of Agadir in a taxi, a mysterious briefcase in my charge.

So I intend to continue going, to try all the different shamis, and the saffron cookies and fresh juices, and await my twist of fate.

Ensorcelled by Mycomancy

I realized today standing next to a homeless man that he smelled like dried mushrooms. Not that he didn't smell bad, or that I didn't find his trail and surround of body odour unpleasant, but the more I thought about it, the more familiar, and undeniably akin to that of dried yellow boletus or morel mushrooms it became. I am no mycologist, but I happen to have both of those mushrooms in my kitchen, dried.

So: earthy, distinctly fungal, slightly sour. It is interesting (or perhaps belaboured to the point of utter banality, although at the moment I find *myself* interested) how tethered are some tastes and smells to context and our own expectations thereof. Obviously, obviously.

If one bites into an apple that tastes like Roquefort, they will spit it out, presumably. And here I am, faced with a smell to whose properties I in other circumstances attribute comfort, richness, even decadence, but in these circumstances I cannot help but wrinkle my nose and seek fresher air (not, I assure you, conspicuously. I do not begrudge the strong-smelling, particularly the strong-smelling homeless, their stink).

I guess that much depends on from where the tiny particulates that are flying up your nose originate, and your attendant associations with them. To have evoked damp leaves, fall forests and the mustiness of the earth is more pleasant than stale, souring sweat and the best-ignored suspicion that this smell too could be related to fungal growth. Although further contemplation yields another turn—perhaps such a smell encountered under other circumstances; in the course of the exploration of another's body, for example, in an armpit or other crevice, is more likely to conjure a fonder association with the delicacy and satisfaction of the food. We can surely see ourselves smiling at the almost-vulgar and shameless, if stylized, honesty of the writer who tenderly describes their lover smelling *"warmly of wine, and mushrooms and rotting pine"* or something. Right?

(I have also noticed that sometimes pasteurized honey reminds me of a cat's butt, if I'm not ready for it.)[1]

---

1 It should of further interest to note that there is an entire family of mushrooms, commonly referred to as "Stinkhorns," that exude the smell of rotting corpses, in order to attract flies and other creatures that feed off of dead flesh. The mushrooms themselves secrete their spores in a sort of viscous goo, that those attracted carry away with them once they have discovered that it's just another goddamn deceitful boner. Did I mention that they also look like slimy dicks? Hence their hilarious Latin name, *Phallus impudicus*, and no, I did not just make that up.

The Appropriate Vanity-Concerning Aphorism is (I Assume) on the Tip of My Tongue

It is folly, I believe, to insist upon the separation of vanity from our enjoyment of food (pretend for a moment that this is *apropos* of anything). It may in fact be more honourable, and more tasteful to consider a meal solely on its own merits and not our associated private pretenses, but I'm having none of it.

I am instead having the experience of my already delicious dinner enhanced by the sense of moral superiority imparted by it also being tremendously healthy. I don't intend to waste anyone's time (oddly enough) prattling on about how I'm not a health snob—I'm not, but in fact a regular junk-food-loving Joe (also inaccurate), and I don't think one needs to atone for their garbage-eating in any self-flagellating fashion, but I have eaten nothing but (a surfeit of) cookies for the past eight hours, and precisely what I need right now is parsnip, rapini, and seeds.[1]

Mashed parsnips, steamed kale, and toasted sunflower seeds—don't think I am unaware that I could not be more stereotypically "why no one takes vegetarians seriously" if I was clad in Whole Foods brand Sackcloth N' Ashes, eating berries and dry grass off the "ground" on my rooftop or-

---

[1] why you should never come to me for recipes:
parsnips: peeled, sliced, boiled, mashed
rapini: thickest stalks removed, steamed (over the boiling parsnips)
walnuts and sunflower seeds: toasted in oven. Add the walnut seeds a couple minutes in, so's they don't bur
seasoning: butter (in mash), olive oil, salt, pepper, squeeze of lemon juice.

ganic garden, but *it be autumn* right now and you all should make a point of not missing out on the cornucopia of hearty vegetable delights currently at your disposal.

See, there's more to autumn than the enjoyment of watching everything turn brittle and die around you, and not only is this shit delicious, but you benefit psychologically from the shameless self satisfaction of enjoying bitter greens and stinky, pungent root vegetables. Party on.

Moreish

Moreish, *adjective* that which makes one desire more.

A late eighteenth century colloquialism that has fallen into disuse (outside of the UK, at least), although it seems to me is ripe for a return to the North American scene at any moment. Rather, it *should* have returned in the '80s or '90s, when this passage from Swift might well have made clever ad copy for a commercial set in a dusty drawing room with a man sporting a bowler hat and comical moustache:

> Lady S.: How do you like this tea, Colonel?
>
> Colonel: Well enough, Madam; but methinks 'tis a little moreish.

> –Jonathan Swift, *Polite Conversation: Consisting of Smart, Whitty, Droll and Whimsical Sayings, Collected for His Amusement, and Made into a Regular Dialogue*, 1783

What I like about this word is that it speaks to an otherwise ineffable quality of food that encourages further indulgence, irrespective of any nutritional value or otherwise life-sustaining properties. And, as far as can be discerned from the OED, unlike delicious, say, moreish makes no claim to this compulsion being a matter of taste or even of pleasure. It brings to mind Walter Benjamin's "I ate to destroy it,"[1] even if the latter describes something closer to a fatal strategy[2] than a something that inheres in the item itself.

1 See "Food As Destroyer."
2 See Jean Baudrillard, *Fatal Strategies* (1990).

I Feel Really Classy Right Now

In the winter of 2009 I, my roommate, and two best friends got it into our heads that "Geez, we should go to Europe, or something," and so Hal, Brendan and myself set out to meet our fourth, Mike, who was recovering from a book tour in Barcelona. The following is an account, transcribed unedited, from my notebook of our flight to Paris. Spelling errors and other unsavouries have been left intact for the sake of the historical record.

I am willing to believe it is somewhere in the vicinity of 1am, and we are (doubtless) suspended, hurtling, over the Atlantic ocean, and I, having just swallowed a lemon pip, am covered in whiskey.

We depend upon the goodwill and spirit of *bonvivance* of the French (authorities) to forgive our Stooge-like and affected blubbering and shrugs of perplexity regarding the whereabouts of the 1.75L of Jameson our boarding pass confirms we purchased at the duty-free, but are inexplicably no longer in possession of.

EUROPA BEGINS.
"It's ... it's ... twenty ... times. Two hundred. No, two fifty."
"Twenty times two fifty."
"No, it's two hundred, it's ... twenty packs of ten cigarettes"
"No, it's ten packs of twenty cigarettes"
"That is the SAME number"
"Ever heard of THAT, Campbell?"

Brendan has just bought two hundred cigarettes off the
flight attendant. The same flight attendant who, just as
improbably, owes Hal 4€.

—

Consistent with the reviews, Julie & Julia is flattened by the
general uninterestingness of the Julie Powell/Amy Adams
portions, which in Ephron style but lacking even the wit
of usual Ephron fare, draws the energy out of the Child/
Streep's story, which is given shorter screentime shrift. All
along one has the suspicion that Julie Powell's story lacks
the dramatic momentum to sustain an entire film, whereas
the cursory and extranarrative/temporal/diagetic portion of
My Life In France feels robbed/barred from occupying the
necessary space to breathe and swell its lungs to requisite
capacity capacitating its merits.

see:

~~inspired by~~
~~consumed by~~

downpressed by thirty is the new twenty malaise—inspired
by Julia Child—decides to write blog (who cares)—blog
becomes book—book—book becomes the movie you're
watching

vs.

downpressed by *midlife* expatriate malaise—*is* Julia Child—
begins cooking in her late thirties—enrolls at the Cordon
Bleu—writes groundbreaking cookbook introducing and
cementing reputation of French cooking in American cul-

ture—becomes landmark TV cooking personality/icon

HAL IS NOW COVERED IN CLUB SODA.
(fact check – tonic water)

Hey, and apparently it ends *before* Julia Child gets her TV show. Boring.

External temperature -52° C, airspeed: 918 km/h, land-speed: unknown.

Hal wishes it to be known we are now west of Greenland.

I prefer to think of us in relation to the Hebrides.

Brendan wishes it be known he is listening to Angel Witch.

Hal, on inspecting the 200 pack of Marlboro's: "There's not much literature on this."

then:

"The Laws Are Not Applicable Over The Waters."

We Are Now Watching Land of The Lost (which apparently exists?) (There is a certain class of movie which I suspect only exists on airplanes. Land of the Lost and Speed Racer have such a distinction) [*note: much of the following consists of quotations from Land of the Lost*]

THERE ARE HUGE AMOUNTS OF TRANSDIMENSIONAL ENERGY OUT THERE WAITING TO BE DIVERTED.

I'm *in control*, and I don't have to go back to feelings.

THIS, instead of Death in Venice... I keep thinking I'm hearing the TWIN PEAKS music.

OKAY, CURRENTLY IN OUR PARTY:
...congratulations, you have just given murderous primates the power of fire.

YOUR LOYALTY IS NOW IN QUESTION!!!

—

DAY 2, 0600h, ZULU TIME.
Breakfast, at a glance, 8h20 Paris time—wretched.
The top of what I assume, through the cellophane grimly, to be a (nonspecifically) "field berry" muffin, is clinging, defoliated/detached [unclear] from the cakebody proper, to its packaging.
oh well.
No curious marzipan (no ital/suisse sweet cheese?) turnover for us.
Just weak tea and this. a fitting upbraid for the state of the soda and Jameson-sodden carpet beneath us.
jus de tomate?
Well, thin tea, muffin and tomato jus, for free isn't so bad.
This is, in fact, a goodly can of tomato juice.
The *"Blonde In Pink Who Loses Her Wallet"* is inspiring a newfound respect for Juste Pour Rire in me. The key/genius lies in its tremendous, disproportionate technical complexity, and stands remarkably/singularly as a JPR gag that does not reveal itself as such (qua _____?... per se!) at the climax of the joke/pageant/performance/process.
Hal: "I just stood in the line for fifteen minutes at the bathroom because this kid pissed his pants and the stewardesses tried to address this by stuffing napkins in his shoes... he's *not wearing any pants*... I don't want to watch this abomination [indistinct]... When the plane lands we're

going to shame that kid like you've never seen a shaming..."

Eight hours later we are looking out over Marseille, eyes bleary but lit from within by a welling fire of excitement. The view afforded from the carré Narvik *train station, perched atop its ornate pedestal of steps, offers up a tumult of twisting alleys, mysterious and picturesque, the horizon a glittering sea. I look forward to an age when I will recall the four of us sitting in the dim at the foot of a great fortress each with our own bottle of insipid* Beaujolais nouveau *through the redemptive mist of nostalgia, rather than the fog of over-the-counter codeine w/caffeine, mutual resentment, and* crise-foie *that quickly settled over Marseille.*

Part Two: Live to Eat

The Chip Returns, Part One

1. "Like a Pizza Chip, but a Pizza that has Chorizo on it."
We ate a lot of chips in Europe. As many and as often as
we could, given the time spent infighting and friendless,
stalking the streets of ancient capitals and dirty dangerous
port towns with our plastic sacks of tiny, watery French
beer and our unslakable thirsts for something worth writing home about.

Unfortunately and paradoxically, as I *am* writing home
about them, after a fashion, Bret's Chorizo chips do not
really qualify.

It is useful in a project such as this, the evaluation of foreign chip flavours, to have already a shared lexicon, as do
those of us who came of age in the Canadian wilds during
the heady days of the Early '90s Chip Flavour Bonanza
(Pizza! Hamburger! Hot dog! Roast turkey and stuffing!
Bacon &... chive or something!). For while the domestic
flavour selection may wax and wane (as I write this we are
at a time of resurgence), we already have these flavour
complexes to work with. However handy as points of reference, there is also the possibility that they may hinder
our ability to break down and properly evaluate what it is
we are tasting.

The canon already does this: salt & vinegar, BBQ,
ketchup, and, to a lesser extent, sour cream 'n' onion and
dill pickle; these are for us the building blocks of what new
flavour profiles we may encounter. But think about how

complex are even these elementary particles! Take the list of ingredients for Ruffles "Authentic BBQ":

> Sugar, Corn Maltodextrin, Dextrose, Brown Sugar, Onion Powder, Monosodium Glutamate, Spices, Salt, Tomato Powder, Molasses Solids, Autolyzed Yeast Extract, Modified Corn Starch, Artificial Color (Including Yellow 5 Lake, Yellow 6 Lake, Blue 2 Lake, Red 40, Yellow 5, Blue 1), Sunflower Oil, Garlic Powder, Corn Starch, Citric Acid, Natural and Artificial Flavors, Natural Mesquite Smoke Flavor, Disodium Inosinate, Disodium Guanylate.

How much is revealed by so hilarious a succession of chemical compounds? The actual organoleptic profile disguises its trail even as the individual components are recorded in the mundane ritual of the ingredient list. For the gestalt is in the end opaque, insoluble. The phenomenal and neuropsychological experiences of so many interacting agents—clustering into identifiable units of taste, progressively accreting in the mind until one has a (somewhat) clear sense of what is meant by "BBQ"—leave us with no idea of how much of this or that went into what it is we are tasting. And yet BBQ as an idea remains not only recognizable, but immanently so across many different manifestations thereof. It is both astonishingly impressive and painfully banal, the sort of shortcuts the brain creates in order to make the perceptual world liveable and endurable.

Which leads to such conversational legerdemain as the following:

"Hm. Not so much, eh?"

"It'd be a pretty good pizza chip, though."

"Yeah, except if it was a pizza chip, you'd still be like, '*this doesn't taste like pizza*.'"

(contemplative pause)

"Well, maybe a pepperoni pizza."

"Yeah, I suppose this *spicy cured meat*-flavoured potato chip *does* maybe taste like a pizza with spicy cured meat on it."

2. Marseilles is Not France, We Are Told, and Its Chips Bewilder.

Ham chips, mon gars!

The *Lay's à l'Ancienne, Jambon Fumée* are, as far as I can tell, the French equivalent of the *Jamón Ruffles* to which I was temporarily addicted in Barcelona last year, and whose unavailability in the New World I have much bemoaned in the time since. Don't ask me how they did it (liquid ham, I'm assuming) but the good Gauls of *Lay's* (Fr.) have swooped to my rescue, here in Marseilles where the Marseillais(es) laugh openly and contemptuously at our pants, and our only defences are our winey constitutions and our Wayfarers.

They really taste almost *too much* like ham.

Other chips we have sampled in Marseilles: *Balsamic Vinegar* that unfortunately just taste kind of like a weak salt and vinegar, which Mike pointed out makes sense, since chips are salty and balsamic is vinegar, but it's a sad sort of sense as these chips certainly lack that distinct taste of, uh, balsa wood or whatever makes balsamic the beloved of *acetos*. We also tried *Moutarde* which basically tasted like a shitty BBQ. Oh well.

However, also on the "perhaps too much like what they're supposed to taste like" side are the *Sibel Black Truffle* chips, which fuck, yeah, really do taste a lot like truffles. It turns out this may not be something I need, after going a

little crazy on the shocking affordability of fresh wild mushrooms here. I paid €3.40 in the damp Arab night-market
for a heaping two handsful of *chanterelles, trompettes de
la mort,* and something orange-capped and green-gilled.
Much to my own disappointment in myself, I don't know
that I can handle more mushrooms. For a day or so at least.
So draws to a close our sojourn in Marseille, and now we
must stay awake until the day threatens to break anew in
order to catch our 5h20 train to Rome, a task for which we
may be forced to enlist the assistance of the energy drink
we bought that advises you to dilute it with seven parts
water before consumption.

Angels of the road, protect us.

Oh, and the other day I ate a lamb heart sandwich just
'cos I could.

3. "Sour Wine on a Sponge."

In Rome, well into a night that had started with "Well,
fuck it, why not?" and progressed through an expensive,
unnecessary crosstown cab ride, the loss of our camera, a
harried and shameful flight from an Italian rock bar, two
encounters with the *Polizia* from which we escaped only by
dint of our apparently sympathetic imbecility, and the inevitable descent into in-group fisticuffs, we found ourselves in
the midst of a heated and insensible argument about the fea-
sibility of swimming across the Tiber. I do not flatter myself
so much as to consider mine the voice of reason; rather that
of cautious pessimism. It is, however, to my credit (if one
may deem a preoccupation with gluttony creditable) that in
the midst of this ill-fated dispute I was able to pipe in with
the following: "Okay guys, hang on a second...What do you
make of these Crik Crok EXTREME Paprika Chips?"

Not much, as it turned out. Nicely crisp, surprisingly spicy, but as with anything with paprika as the dominant flavour, disappointing; although they did divert our attention sufficiently to prevent any of us from joining our destinies to those of the criminals and poor Popes who met their restless tumbling ends in the embrace of the river. *Potaverunt me aceto*, but the steady hand of the chip prevails.

Brassica Uber Alles, Part One:
Chouette First, Ask Questions Later?

It is a fixture of my insufferableness that if, when embarking publicly on an analysis of some quibbling feature of language or social reality, I am met with skepticism and (supposed) indifference so fervently avowed as to border on the venomous, I take it as an indication that I am on the right path, and my resolve is strengthened accordingly.

You know, I'm like "Hey, you ever think about how blah blah blah?" and they're all like "that's stupid, who cares, please shut up," and so, inevitably I'm all "Whoa ho, methinks thou dost protest too much!" and I become even more interested in whatever the fuck it is—cabbages or something. I mean, it's a vulgar psychoanalytic trick and basically Zizek's equivalent of the People's Elbow, but I think there is often enough something to it to justify my taking what may be merely an annoying habit/personality defect as a point of personal pride.

In this case, yes, it is cabbages, thank you very much; more specifically the currency and polysemic richness of *chou* (cabbage) in the French language.

I got to thinking about this after I had my first (first! I know!) *petit chou* at a bakery in Paris (not a bad place to start, though). In this case, the *chou à la crème*, effectively a cream puff, (effectively, *the best* cream puff, holy shit), is so-called because it resembles more or less a cabbage, and has nothing else to do with cabbage than that; just as chocolate truffles are so named because of their loose resemblance to fungus truffles, and for no other reason. The immediate question that arises is, "why cabbage?" the answer to which, of course, is, "shut the fuck up," and I'd be happy to leave it at that if that was where it ended (because they do look more or less like little cabbages), but it so happens that *chou* is a very popular and versatile word.

The dough itself from which *chou à la crème are made is called pâte à choux*, a light, egg-based pastry dough that originally (albeit perhaps apocryphally?) derives its name from the cabbagey-looking buns (distinct from modern-day *chou*? It remains unclear) made by the nineteenth century master pastry chef Jean Avice.

Chou itself refers, as does cabbage, to both the family, *brassica/cruciferae*, and the species, *oleracea*, but to a greater extent than the English, it permeates the nomenclature of its relatives and its preparations. See: *chou-fleur, choux de Brux-elles, chou frisé, chou-rave, choucroute* (cauliflower, Brussels sprouts, kale, kohlrabi, sauerkraut), where the *chou*/cabbage occupies the seat, within its field, of ontological primacy.

But is it merely within its field? My whole train of consid-eration was set off by hearing *chou* used as a term of endear-ment—like *ma blonde, mon chou/ma choute* is a *Québecois* expression for boyfriend/girlfriend. Further, *chou* can also operate as an adjective (familiar, of course) meaning nice, cute, generally sweet; as does *chouette* which, complicating things further, also means *owl*, and, WTF, can refer casually to a random object, as might thinger or whatchamajigget! So what came first, the owl or the cabbage? And why are cabbages so cute? AND WHY DO THE FRENCH LOVE CABBAGES SO? For, as it turns out, it persists still further and farther afield in the French idiom.

In my *Petit Larousse* alone I came up with "*aller planter ses choux*," ("Go plant his cabbage") meaning to retire to the country; "*bête comme chou*," ("silly/simple/stupid like a cabbage") for something that's really easy; "*faire ses choux gras*" ("to fatten his cabbages"), meaning to capitalize on something; "*feuille de chou*" ("cabbage leaf"), for a crappy newspaper; "*être dans les choux*"[1] ("to be in the cabbages"), and "*faire chou blanc*" ("to make white cabbage"? Maybe "to whiten one's cabbage"? Perhaps refers to overcooking a cabbage?[2]), for being fucked/in a fucked situation, and to totally fuck something up/fail, respectively; and "*bout de choux*" (the "tip or bud of a cabbage"), for a small child.

See what I'm saying? I mean, I'm not saying that there is some sinister ideological undercurrent to the ubiquity of the word, but I am curious how it came to be so prevalent and diversely employed. Particularly because we Anglos certainly do not seem to give the cabbage much play. It's a much maligned vegetable, and when we stop to think about it, which is rarely, it tends to conjure associations with poverty and commonness. A fine instance of this can be found in MFK Fisher's "The Social Status of a Vegetable" (*Harper's*, April 1937):

> At the word spinach her face clouded, but when I mentioned cabbage a look of complete and horrified

---

1 A cook friend of mine has commented that she had always in Québecois kitchens heard "*dans le jus*" ("In the juice/sauce"). It is unclear whether this literally intended to be "in the juice," or whether it is derived from "*dans le chou*." They both seem equally plausible.

2 It has since been brought to my attention that the expression in fact derives from the expression "*faire coup blanc*" (euh, "make a white strike?"), which means to manage to not score a single point in nine-pin bowling. "*Chou*" is supposedly a regional pronunciation of "coup." Still more confusing because of the opposite meanings of "strike" in French and English bowling contexts, although I guess it's good to know that the French also bowl, a fact of which I had no idea.

disgust settled like a cloud. She pushed back her chair.

"Cabbage!" Her tone was incredulous.

"Why not?" James asked mildly, "Cabbage is the staff of life in many countries. You ought to know, Mrs. Davidson. Weren't you raised on a farm?"

Her mouth settled grimly.

"As *you* know," she remarked in an icy voice, with her face gradually looking very old and discontented again, "there are many kinds of farms. My home was *not* a collection of peasants. Nor did we eat such—such peasant things as this."

[...]

"Why do you really dislike cabbage, Mrs. Davidson?"

She looked surprised, and put down the last bite of her bowl of brandied plums.

"Why does anyone dislike it? Surely you don't believe that I think your eating it is anything more than a pose?" She smiled knowingly at her nephew and me.

This is great, because it's like the *very idea* of eating cabbage is offensive. The older woman goes on, after some prodding, to share her experience of being totally traumatized to see how her future husband lived, from what sad and squalid origins he came, ramshackle slums where the scent of boiled cabbage hung everywhere in the air. It's fully worth reading the whole article, as is invariably the case with Fisher (who now crowns my list of People For Whom I Should Probably Invent A Time Machine For The Purposes of Seducing/Being Seduced By), I assure you.

Following the above, if the French had only negative cabbage-invoking expressions, one could make a more simplistic claim about the ideological embeddedness of language, food, etc., but it is precisely how *chou* resists such an explanation that intrigues me. For that matter, I do not even know whether cabbage has the same class connotations in France as in England. It is a rough, hardy fare, but my patchy knowledge (i.e. total ignorance) of European agricultural history could afford me only the most amateurish and intellectually irresponsible generalizations about language and alimentary materialism, so for the moment I must refrain.

Waverley Root, at least, has suggested that the prestige of cabbage has oscillated wildly across cultures and throughout history; the Greeks, not so much ("If you lived on cabbage, you would not be obliged to flatter the powerful," said Diogenes, "If you flattered the powerful," his young friend replied "you would not be obliged to live on cabbage."[3]), but for the Romans it fetched an exorbitant price and was the favourite of many an Emperor. He also writes that it was the French royal chef Taillevent who should be honoured with bringing vegetables back onto the tables of the Middle Ages, by way of a preparation of cabbage at a banquet of Charles VI. This unfortunately brings us no closer to the past two hundred years, which I think are what really count (besides religious pro/prescriptions) for shaping cultural attitudes about modern food.

Even if there is no *reason* per se for this cruciferous predilection, and it should prove to be the essence of happenstance that the French have been so fundamentally romanced by the sound and the spirit of the cabbage, if not necessarily the taste, I find that no less interesting.

Oh, cabbages. Your drama will unfold.

---

3 From *Food: An Authoritative Visual History and Dictionary of the Foods of the World* (1980)

Deipnosophist

Deipnosophist, *noun* one learned in the mysteries of the kitchen, a master of the art of dining.

Don't let anyone tell you that a deipnosophist is someone who is skilled at the art of dinner conversation (which it is), because what it *really* (i.e. *also*) means is someone who is a master of the art of dining itself, of which conversation is but one of many facets, damn it.

I was once accused of sophistry (only once? I know!), on a bus in effing fucking Barcelona, and it's stuck with me ever since, particularly as I feel it was somewhat unfair. However, had the accusation been of deipnosophy, I would have been elated!

Although, had deipnosophy the same pejorative connotations as sophistry, but with a dinnerary bent, I would not feel elated at all, but rather defeated and quite as if someone had my number. I am absolutely a student and lover of dinner, but if we take all aspects into account, I am pretty bad at it. I can't maintain conversation while cooking, I often mismatch food and wine, and almost without exception eat to the point of crapulent self-hatred.

One would think that so essential and regularly practiced a skill as feeding oneself would be easy to keep honed to a fine point, but apparently I have shit the bed on that one, because I can't even eat good.

Caute, Capparis

Up until very recently our house was well stocked with caperberries. This fairly unlikely state of affairs was brought about by a cohort of mine having one afternoon stumbled upon an unattended delivery truck behind a gourmet foods store and—in what I am sure was a paroxysm of harried acquisitiveness shot through with incredulous gratitude at such good fortune—subsequently come out of it in possession of a very large, very nice jar of Dijon mustard, two bottles of *cidre pétillant* (I am of the impression that in spite of living in a province where *all* things are labeled in French, should something be above a certain price, one is simply *verboten* to translate it, golly. We are not hill people after all; discernment is not beyond us), and a case of what turned out to be *caperberries*.

Much to his personal discomfiture, it turns out he despises the things, whereas I, happily, do not.

Fast-forward two or three years and find me finally dispatching the last of the twenty-four bottles, a couple of which I admit I did not personally see to, but passed on to interested or merely curious parties. If you're unfamiliar, caperberries are very much like capers, and in fact come from the same plant *capparis spinosa*, but whereas the capers we know are the immature buds thereof, caper*berries* are as the name implies the berry or fruiting body. They have a similar faintly mustardy taste, either more or less pungent depending on who you ask, and are about the size of a biggish red grape, with a little stem. Some are off-put by the occasional unexpected presence of crunchy little seeds inside, but I think they are easily managed if you see them coming. Do not feel abashed if you've never encountered them; it is a rarity that anyone to whom I speak of them has. Approximately as rare, I trust, as is the experience on the other hand of being confronted by someone who insists on talking to you about caperberries, to say nothing of sending you home with a jar of your own.

They must not be very popular.

———

Perhaps the only instance, in fact, in which I have come across them in my day-to-day, and which I realize tonight always springs to mind when I am asking myself at what point to add the caperberries to whatever it is that I am making, is that scene in *Hannibal* where Anthony Hopkins feeds Ray Liotta part of his own brain, lightly sautéed in butter with shallots and, yeah, caperberries.

There is a long tradition associating culinary refinement with moral corruption, indeed all refinement that eschews asceticism for sensuality, and short of actually getting into it (because brother, I could *go on*), I'll say that my interest has been piqued recently by Christianity's (very uneven, granted) history of positing a zero-sum relationship between the promise of the afterlife and the at times heretical audacity to enjoy the earth's bounty whilst in and of it.

Hannibal, of course, is the aesthete *par excellence*, or arguably *ad absurdum*, separated by mere decrements of humanity from Dorian Gray in his descent into the pleasures of the flesh. And I see it as a means of imposing a still greater remove that Thomas Harris has Lecter use caperberries in lieu of the perhaps more accessible, more familiar *caper*, in his preparation.

His cannibalistic gastronomy, or to put a finer point on it, the *epicureanism* of his cannibalism, becomes the haunting, "unhealthy"[1] detail in which the devil figuratively resides.

Okay, I take that back—the Dorian Gray comparison, at least. Which I know means I could just not write it at all, but I feel like it is a point worth making, rhetorically, in order to provide a pretext for the correction—Hannibal Lecter is actually wildly[2] different from Dorian Gray, in that unlike the typical aesthete, and certainly the dandy, Lecter's concern with beauty is meant to be complex, negotiated and *profound*, as opposed to affected or superficial. Jonathan Romney calls him "a nightmare mix between Ted Bundy and George Steiner," which makes the point, if being a bit of a stretch in my opinion, because I can't ever imagine Steiner being so smug an SOB as Lecter, even though he's probably got every right. Maybe the smugness is Bundy? And the murdering? Anyhoo, whereas Dorian Gray is fairly literally putrefied from the inside out by his excessive preoccupation with artifice and sensual pleasure, there is a sense with Lecter (which as I understand it is fleshed out more explicitly in the Harris's Hannibal novels than in their somewhat uneven film adaptations) that he is *completed* by his interest in beauty. It is his capacity for evil that allows him to be *truer to beauty*—remember that he (mostly) kills and eats only the annoying and vulgar, and through cuisine makes something beautiful and refined of them, before incorporating them, thus being both literally and spiritually nourished by this interest in beauty. Right? Weird.

---

1 Unhealthy in the colloquial sense, of course—mere cannibalism is crazy and horrifying, but the care and discernment Hannibal devotes is what is truly disturbed and disturbing.

2 Okay, I know I talk trash on indiscriminate punning, but that was totally unintentional, or at least unconscious.

Quaff While Thou Canst

Will Smith: "Cheers, *skaal, prost!*"
The Other Guy: "Mud in your eye."
from Six Degrees of Separation (1993)

Why has this exchange stuck in my mind? There should be nothing particularly memorable about it, and yet every time glasses are raised in common it is the first thing to go through my mind. I do have a soft spot for conspicuous refinement, particularly when part of an artful dissemblance[1], as opposed to a mere shabby pretense, and I am interested in toasts, cheers, and health-drinking (both the ritual verbalizing and the practical knocking back) but the latter interest is a more recent phenomenon. In fact, I cannot assure myself that my interest in cheersing was not precipitated by the peculiar insistence with which the above quotation wormed into my brain.

Perhaps it is because I had no idea what the two toasts meant until very recently. It is easy to infer of course, as they are toasts, but toasts to what, and of what order and origin?

---

1 If you haven't seen *Six Degrees of Separation*, I heartily recommend it, and suggest you don't read the current sentence wherein I reveal that Will Smith plays a gay con man. There's a really interesting interplay of class, race and sexuality, shot through with what I think is a partly unintentional analysis of boundary maintenance and the linked symbolic hierarchies of criminality and mental illness, but it ends up being a movie that seems to skewer and negate its most poignant insight mere moments after articulating it. I choose to believe that the play ends on a less confused note.

Well, *prost* or *prosit* is a common German or Austrian toast, which like most gives us a rough "to your health!" and apparently derives from the Latin *prosit*, meaning "let it benefit." I'd heard this around, and most whom I asked about it were at least familiar.

"(Here's) mud in your eye!" is one I've long enjoyed, but which has seemed ambiguous—it has a ring of good-natured ribbing to it, equally at home in the mouth of a dyed-in-the-wool Midwestern farmhand or some brassy trollop from a 1940s screwball comedy.

Like most colloquialisms, it is difficult to sort out exactly when and where and how it came into use, but it has been suggested to have a Biblical origin. John 9:6 has Jesus putting mud in the eye of a blind man to heal him, which resonates with the strange way that what sounds like an insult is actually a cheers: saying, "here's mud in your eye" seems like a diss, as having mud in your eye seems like a bad thing, but lo, it actually is a cry to your health, just as the mud turned out to be beneficial (in the right hands). You are effectively interpellated into the position of the blind man who will be made to see, ironically, through booze.

Interestingly, this is the very same blind man responsible for the familiar refrain "I once was blind, but now I see." The whole passage reads "I do not know that he was a sinner. One thing I do know, that I once was blind but now I see" (9:26), referring to the fact (well, you know, "fact") that Jesus was regarded by the Pharisees as a sinner for having performed a healing on the Sabbath. Which can be interpreted further, for our purposes, as a means of justifying drinking on Sundays. For those of us who feel it makes them more colourful to provide elaborate and suspect justifications for things, "it may seem like a bad idea, but this is a balm. I once was blind, but now I have had six mimosas, as is God's will."[2]

Etymologically speaking, things really start to heat up when we get to *skaal* or *skoal*. A Scandinavian toast generally understood as "to your health," which is supposed to derive from the motion of raising your cup (circular, that), *skaal/skoal* being Old Norse for "bowl or cup."

A curious note in the Wiktionary entry on *skål* (or *skàl*), describes it as the imperative of *skale*, which could be understood (infinitively) as "to toast," or "to cheer ones health." So what seems to have happened is we start with a noun, the bowl (*skaal*), which is then verbed by being used to do something, to cheers, and then over time the meaning of the action (the cultural meaning of the action) comes to displace the object that is employed, the thing itself becomes the "cheers," not the bowl. This new word then comes to acquire the other grammatical extensions and accoutrement of the verb, until what was originally a noun re-emerges as a particular mood (in the grammatical sense) of the verb? Does this make sense? I admit that it has something of the Conan Doyle about it, but it seems plausible.

In the interest of thickening the plot, and gratifying my own preoccupation with homophony and heavy metal, I can't help thinking about the similarity of this word to our own "skull," particularly when one gets to thinking about the use of the skull as cup, which all sorts of tough-ass peoples have been reputed to do, historically. For "skull," the OED gives the following: "Of obscure origin: first prominent in south-western texts of the 13th-14th centuries, usually in the form *scolle*." A foreign origin is indicated by the initial *sc-*, *sk-*, but the locality of the early examples is

---

2 Side note: don't ever put beer, or let beer be put, into your eyes. It is in fact not a literal balm, I can tell you from experience. In fact, it burns.

against connection with Old Norse *skoltr*...or with Norwegian dialect *skul, skol* shell (of nuts or eggs). There is correspondence of form with Dutch *schol, schulle, scholle*, earthy crust, turf, piece of ice (cf. also Swedish *skolla*, metal plate), but there is no evidence that these were ever used in the sense of 'skull'. The same difficulty applies to Old French *esculle, escule*, dish, nor would this have readily assumed the early form *scolle.*

Which, for our purposes, is the lexicographical equivalent of an exaggerated shrug. So what of the phonic similarity between *skaal* and *skolle*? Is this mere happenstance? Coincidence? Are we to believe that the word *skaal* which sounds like our skull and is the word for cup or bowl, a purpose to which human heads were notoriously if only occasionally put, is in no way responsible for us calling a skull a skull now? Or that the Old Norse words *skalli* (skull) and *skål* (bowl) are only coincidentally, you know, the *same word*?

I wish I had an etymologist friend to pester with questions like these, but I'm pretty sure that this fictional personage is just as relieved that they don't exist and have to deal with me calling them up at two am asking about skull cups and Will Smith movies.

On a more whimsical note, Lord Byron apparently had a skull cup, the lucky skunk (although it was dug up in his garden, not rent from the body of a literary rival or unsympathetic critic, lamentably). He and his buddies "used to sit up late... drinking burgundy, claret, champagne and what not, out of the skull cup, buffooning all around the house in our unconventional garments."[3] Oh, for the carefree, romantic days of the early nineteenth century!

---

3 From a letter to John Murray, November 12th, 1820. *The Letters and Journals of Lord Byron, With Notices of His Life*, by Thomas Moore (1830).

And upon it, bless his soul, a poem:

Lines Inscribed Upon A Cup Formed
From A Skull (1808)

Start not—nor deem my spirit fled
In me behold the only skull,
From which unlike a living head,
Whatever flows is never dull.
I lived, I loved, I quaffed like thee
I died; let earth my bones resign
Fill up—thou canst not injure me;
The worm has fouler lips than thine.
Better to hold the sparkling grape,
Than nurse the earth—worm's slimy brood
And circle in the goblet's shape
The drink of Gods, than reptile's food.
Where once my wit, perchance, hath shone,
In aid of others let me shine;
And when, alas ! our brains are gone,
What nobler substitute than wine?
Quaff while thou canst, another race
When thou and thine, like me, are sped
May rescue thee from earth's embrace
And rhyme and revel with the dead.

At the risk of becoming still more annoying a fop than I already am, I'd love to learn that by heart (my disinterest in poetry warring with my love for verbosity and skulls), but I shan't, don't worry. I shall, however, continue to fantasize that one day I will be able to rely that some bosom friend will respond to my own "Cheers, *skaal, prost*" with a hearty "Mud in your eye."

Petecure

Petecure, *noun* modest cooking, cooking on a small scale (contrasted w/ epicure).

My initial excitement over so delicate and intentional a term of opposition to *epicure* was dampened somewhat upon actually thinking about it, and coming to the conclusion that the resemblance between them was incidental rather than essential. Epicure/epicurean is derived from the man, or at least the followers of the man, *Epikouros.* Although it would be a delightful flourish of mythological symmetry for petecure to have similar origins[1], it in fact comes from Old French: *petite keurie/queurie.* Think *cuire,* to cook, and *petite,* small. What this presents, however, is a more curious phonic convergence that dissembles a family relation. Knowing that they derive from such distinct origins, it is astonishing how friendly and alike are these twinned and opposite terms, epicure and petecure. I'm sure linguists have a word for this, but it always brings to mind for me the phenomenon of convergent evolution in biology, whereby structures of similar form and function are arrived at via very different evolutionary paths (bird wings and bat wings, being in an emotional relationship with a living being and watching too much television, etc.). It is an imperfect analogy, but hey, it's an imperfect world.

---

1 We are to imagine that Petekurous ate mostly wasa crackers and meat tea, I suppose?

Suffice to say it's this kind of thing that gets under my skin and drives home the vast incomprehensibility of the cosmos much more than the usual coincidental and serendipitous bullshit. I could almost start believing in some forgetful and capricious divinity, but I feel like it would turn out to be one of those "kneel and you will believe, or maybe you won't, or maybe you will, but a while later" situations.

"Never Again"
is What You Swore, the Time Before

Nothing draws attention to the delicacy of balance of disparate elements like a succession of unnecessary spin-offs wherein such balance is clumsily dispensed with.

As in the case of the Reese's Peanut Butter Bar. Similar in basic structure to a Caramilk—chocolate chambers filled with, you know, filling—but resembling nothing so much as the generic "Chocolate Bar" of comic books and clipart, there is something fundamentally aesthetically satisfying about the Reese's Peanut Butter Bar. It *looks* classic. But not good. I mean, not awful, but really just not right. Not right in one's head. You can't really hold it against them, because such is the nature of the beast, and chocolate bar novelty marketing can be kind of cute in a sad way, because you'd think that they, if anyone, should have a well established sense of what about their product works and why. But no, those flavour scientists and stuffed-suit junior execs seem to miss the boat a good sixty percent of the time.

We all remember the grotesquerie of the BizarroCup, which if you don't (because probably, you really don't), was the Reese's cup where the peanut butter was on the outside, with a chocolatey filling within.

Beyond the already unsettling suspicions about what one has to do to turn peanut butter into a container, the fundamental flaw of this Cronenbergian abomination was the *sweetening* of the peanut butter, thus disrupting the interplay of savoury and sweet so necessary to the success of the peanut butter cup/most of Thailand.

The mini cups (remember when those were like fifteen cents?) were surprisingly successful, despite an apparently higher p.b.:choc ratio, and conversely, so too are the Big Cups, which, at a whopping thirty-nine grams (it looks and eats bigger than it sounds, trust me), I was ready to write off. Oh, and I mean "successful" in terms of embodying a good thingness/ideal relationship (i.e. tasting good, succeeding at being a Reese's Peanut Butter Cup, as we understand the Reese's Peanut Butter Cup), not so much a commercial success that would turn the Big Cup into a candy aisle mainstay, because I've noticed the Big Cup is not all that easy to find. It's a little nauseating of course, in a way that I think has more to do with a psychic affront to our sense of proportion (resulting in disorder to the faculties) than anything else, because the Big Cup sure disorders you in a way that three normal cups do not. But at least you feel like you've really *done something* with your day.

And then you have this bar thing, which we knew from the outset was a pretty bad idea, but a man's gotta write, right? Again, I think that a big part of the failure is owed to the sweet-savoury being out of whack (the chocolate connective tissue between the cells results in too high a mediocre chocolate content), but what has struck me still more is the textural factor. It seems incredibly obvious in retrospect, but as with all that one takes for granted, the absence of the acute-angle ridges on the periphery radically affects the whole deal. Possibly of parallel importance to the sweet-savoury ratio, which I never would have believed until I experienced first-hand is the honestly disturbing *smoothness* of the Reese's Bar.

And therein lies the awful. Or not quite. And *from there*

proceeds the awful. Because it is not the bar itself that is bad, but it makes you *feel* bad. It is what is missing from these rounded corners that, once apprehended, settles like a cloud of unease over your consciousness, how the absence of a birthmark on a body under exploration shocks you into the sort of dull, low-level ache of the realization that you are cheating with someone you don't even really like, even if no one will ever know.

Does anyone else ever get the impression, reading things like that, of some delicate piece of mechanics, like a sewing machine, which has been dropped and now the thread tension is just horribly skewed? Because I feel fine.

Reese's Peanut Butter bar: 2/5 stars

Boiled Offerings?
What do I Look Like, a Minor Divinity?

> Boiled food is life, roast food is death. Folklore
> the world over offers countless examples of the
> cauldron of immortality; but there is no indica-
> tion anywhere of a spit of immortality.
>
> - Claude-Lévi-Strauss,
> *The Origin of Table Manners* (1978)

Having delved no further than the brief excerpt containing
this quote in Kurlansky's *Choice Cuts* anthology, I find this
curious. Perhaps the anthropological record bears it out,
but presents quite the opposite attitude to my own, if I
think about it. Which I did, just now.

I tend to associate boiling with lifelessness, dissipa-
tion—the draining away of colour, juice, vitality into the
boiling liquid. Roasting, on the other hand, evokes for me
the sealing in, the concentration of flavour, heat, richness,
under a layer of heat-reflecting oil, char, or caramelized
tissue. I boil food as little as possible, with the exception of
grains and the like, and I roast food as a luxury, as often as
time permits. Roasting seems to call the food to create an
armour around itself, it forces in, instead of drawing out. I
see it thus as a matter of interiorizing v. exteriorizing, and it
is clear which of these I find attractive.

But my language betrays itself. For what of the above
description of boiling is inconsistent with immortality?
Put more precisely, my thoughts about roasting and boil-

ing actually correspond to two different schools of thought about immortality, and particularly the (im/possible) role of selfhood therein. In many (mystic, not exclusively eastern) traditions immortality is conceptualized as just that sort of dissipation/disintegration into the surrounding waters—the return of one's life energy to the perhaps undifferentiated cosmic glop, the end of the self, effectively . But is this immortality or is it (mere) death? When in *The Black Hole* (1979) Dr. Reinhardt fantasizes about passing into and through the black hole, he imagines entering a realm without and beyond death, but seemingly not beyond life; he hopes to claim an immortality for himself, a limitless knowledge, but still believes that he will persist as a knower, as a life, as opposed to being consumed, subsumed into this knowledge.[1]

Roasting, I suppose, recalls this position—an idea of immortality that is a sort of concentration of life inside the self, inside a body or at least loosely within the contours of a consciousness—*the condensation of (a) life* as opposed to its disintegration. The life is toughened against the ravages of time, not integrated into its warp and weft.

In this respect, it is Lévi-Strauss's mingling of Life v. Death with talk of Immortality that puts me in a bit of a muddle. Immortality v. what? Mortality, presumably? But Life-Death is not the same dialectic as Immortality-Mortality. Life and Death are under the purview of Mortality—Mortality is the condition that *allows* Life, just as it *guarantees* Death, Immortality is the opportunity to opt out of the conversation entirely, in a sense. Assuming that we mean something different from Immortality when we

---

1 You have no idea how hotly and how tirelessly my roommate and I debated the ultimate significance of this movie, made for children thirty-two years ago.

say "I Want To Live Forever," which clearly I was, but perhaps it is not a safe assumption to make.

"A rite performed by the Cree Indians of Canada conveys very clearly the *cosmic totality attributed to boiled food*," Lévi-Strauss again. What remains ambiguous, however, is wherein the lies the immortality? Who or what becomes immortal? In *The Physiology of Taste*, Brillat-Savarin speaks of the lowness and unfitness for consumption of the *bouilli*: the piece of meat that is boiled in order to produce a nourishing, savoury *bouillon*. Here, through boiling the meat becomes part of something bigger and better than itself, but in the process really *loses* itself. Now does this literal transcendence of the flesh belong, symbolically, to the register of immortality or to that of death?

Perhaps the intensification of life that I am inclined to see in roasting is just the imprint of human hubris, the egoistic misunderstanding of the promise and very premise of immortality as the perpetuation of the bounded self. Thus the "spit of immortality" is in the end but the lathe of heaven, a connection I will admit I first drew based only on superficial resemblance, but upon consideration is actually quite apposite.

Hrm.

Well, have fun with your *boiled garlic*, you bunch of life-lovers. If you need me, I'll be in flavour country, *with the skeletons*.

Killcrop

Killcrop, *noun* an insatiate brat, popularly thought to be a fairy that has been substituted for the genuine child.

I can only assume that this sort of rationale was meant to serve as a defense against charges of infanticide, along the lines of "you can't blame me, that wasn't even my kid, that was some manner of... interloping hobgoblin."

Anyway, love that word.

Who Is Farinata?

As opposed to "What is farinata?" which is what usually happens when I say things like, "Man, I've been really into farinata lately," or "Have you ever had farinata?" or "Hey, you want to come over for some farinata?" Because no one seems to know what it is, and for that matter, nor did I, until I ran across a recipe for it one day and was like, "Hey, that seems just like socca."

The plot thickens, I know.

So to clarify, after the orgy of comma-spattered obfuscation that is customary around here, we must go to Nice, France of all places.

The fall of 2008 quite improbably found me aboard a cruise ship in the Mediterranean sea, and one of our ports of call was *Villefranche-Sur-Mer*. Where, as there is little to do besides see Cocteau's chapel (closed) and, you know, enjoy the *French fucking Riviera*, we decided to hop the train over to Nice, which we heard was okay. And I'm happy we did; happier still that my traveling companion had the wherewithal to learn a little about the place beforehand, because as a result we spent much of our day wending our way down circuitous streets in search of what the four pages I had torn out of some past-due Lonely Planet assured us was a must-try of Niçoise cuisine—socca. If you're as confused as I was by the distinctly un-French sounding name you shall remain so because I have yet to sort out its origins. You may be still further confused by the fact that it's basically made out of chickpea flour and olive oil—not exactly the first ingredients that spring to mind when one thinks of staples of French cuisine. Socca is a chickpea flour-based sort of flatbread-*cum*-crêpe that has a faintly fermented taste and is cooked on ginormous pans in big wood-fired ovens. It is a street food and therefore 1) greasy as fuck, and 2) delicious. Where we ended up, thanks to the directions of the native Niçois and Nicoises we hassled ("Keep going down this way, and you'll see so-and-so's socca, but don't go there, you got to keep going, to such and such other place, for the real, the best socca in Nice," is a faithful paraphrase.) was a big lunch counter type joint in an old stone building (of course) that consisted of an open kitchen dominated by the aforementioned giant ovens and staffed by an assortment of beautiful/young and old/indestructible Frenchwomen who scraped piles of blistering hot socca onto paper plates for you, along with various other snacks (sardines, cod beignets) and maybe some tartar sauce, depending on your order. The establishment had no seating proper, but for the price of a drink you were welcome to have a seat at one of tables of the apparently unaffiliated bar of nonetheless the same name (which escapes me) directly across the street (a distance of not more than seven feet). At as generous portions of beer and chilled rosé for three euros you'll ever find, I can't recommend it enough, if only I could remember any of the details required for a proper recommendation.[1]

---

1 This is also where I first tried *pissaladière*, which is the *Niçois/Provençal/Ligurian* (apparently) pizza or sometimes puff pastry topped with caramelized onions, olives and anchovies, and is probably one of my Favourite Things. Also another example of defining elements of a dish being left by the wayside in subsequent permutations (see also "Refrain, if at all Possible from Calling it 'Baba G'"). Anchovies specifically, which I am happy leaving out of/off of my *pissaladière*, despite the very name deriving from *pissalat*, a type of anchovy paste—itself derived from the latin *piscis* for fish. Take that, small fry.

Farinata is effectively the same thing as socca, except made by Italians, and more likely to involve rosemary. *And*, hold onto your ever-loving hats, when I made it for the first time at home, it tasted—I swear to god—exactly like KFC skin.

WHOAAAAAAAAAAAAAAAAAAAAAAAAAAAAAAA AM I RIGHT? Well, I know I'm right about the skin thing, because it was the two other people with me at the time who put their fingers on it. But if you're the type of fool who finds the idea of KFC skin repulsive (or to be fair, finds the *reality* repulsive because skin-eating is kind of weird, but we all know that KFC skin is delicious, in *reality*), don't worry about it, just put it out of your head because I guarantee you that this crap is delicious. So here's a recipe, from... I really don't remember, sorry. And it's all in metric, which is useless to me since I don't own a kitchen scale, and if the "tastes like KFC skin" was what sold you, chances are you don't own one either, no offense, but it's pretty convertible if you're comfortable with wingin' it.

300 g chick pea flour
(this is easy to find at Middle Eastern grocery stores)
1L tepid water
1 tsp fresh ground black pepper
1 tbsp sea salt
110 mL olive oil

Carefully whisk flour into a small amount of water so as to avoid lumps, add salt and pepper, then let sit for somewhere between two and twenty-four hours. Skim the foam off the top of the batter and discard, then add the olive oil. Next take a cast iron skillet (with an oven-proof handle, because that's where it's goin'), pour on about one tablespoon olive oil, and throw it (just the pan) into a 450º oven until the oil is just beginning to smoke. Remove skillet, pour in batter so as to create a thin layer, and replace in oven for about ten minutes, till the top is browning and the edges crispy, but the middle still a little soft. You can also top it with fresh rosemary leaves.

This recipe is for a pretty huge batch, so using my giant brain, I converted it roughly into something like a three to one water to flour ratio, with around one tablespoon olive oil per cup water as a general, necessarily tweakable-to-taste guideline. You can cut the oil for a slightly less overwhelming snack, more suited to flatbread-type activities, like scooping up other good things, and my gluten-intolerant friends with whom I have shared this recipe tell me that they have increased the flour-water ratio so as to achieve some serviceable substrate for pizza in order to brighten somewhat their miserable gluten-free lives.

Having sorted that out, to get back to the original question, where does all this "*who*" nonsense come from? Well, leafing through C.S. Lewis' *Screwtape Proposes A Toast* (sequel to *The Screwtape Letters*, wherein we find Screwtape in his natural habitat, making a toast at the dinner of the school of lesser demons), this passage where Screwtape mourns the meager fare that contemporary sinners make, caught my eye:

"Oh, to get one's teeth again into a Farinata, a Henry VIII, or even a Hitler! There was real crackling there; something to crunch; a rage, an egotism, a cruelty only just less robust than our own. It put up a delicious resistance to being devoured. It warmed your inwards when you'd got it down."

Who could this Farinata be, I asked myself, so diabolical as to share a spotlight with Henry VIII and Hitler? Could he be the namesake of my beloved snack? And if so, what dark secrets might teem behind its greasy veil? What ignominy?! As it turns out Farinata the man, Farinata degli Uberti, is of no discernible relation to Farinata the snack. An Italian noble and anti-papist who did some anti-papist stuff (political conniving, I guess? It's all Greek to me, this Roman stuff), but more importantly, disbelieved in the afterlife and, according to Boccaccio, "maintained that happiness consisted in temporal pleasures... was fond of good and delicate viands, and ate them without waiting to be hungry; and for this sin he is damned as a Heretic in this place." Not only damned, he and his wife had their bodies exhumed and *burned* by Inquisition goons as a sort of punishment for heresy by *posthumous execution*, which is basically the most fascinating, blasted thing I've heard all day. An "it is not enough that justice be done, justice must be seen to be seen to be done" sort of thing, like the effing wicked *Cadaver Synod* of a.d. 897, where the corpse of Pope Formosus was disinterred, placed on trial, condemned for whatever and then ceremoniously unceremoniously dumped in the Tiber. It would be something of a comfort if the wages of such sins of indulging in temporal pleasures and delicate viands (as I do) were to be paid only in the form of corpse desecration, rather than the bloating and hangovers which I must suffer daily in this mortal coil.

Farinata, the dude, makes an appearance in *The Divine Comedy* too (you know, in Hell); but all this still seems thin grounds for his soul to serve as such substantial fare for demons as Hitler, say. However, if one accepts the absurdity that enjoyment of the feast of the senses should be a sin

(God's Work being Good and all), then feasting itself may then be viewed as a sort of statement of rejection. A statement more profound if not made simply by an isolated lapse of judgment one rainy night at a Boston Red Lobster, but rather by a whole lifestyle based on the rejection of, or even the *indifference to* what God has to offer-spiritual immortality being the big fifty-two cent carrot.

Excuse me while I go eat an entire pizza.

Lessons Not So Much Learned
As Accumulated, Like Stretch
Marks of the Spirit

If ever we took seriously our New Year's resolutions, at least those uttered with the greatest frequency and conviction in the first forty-eight hours of the new year, we would none of us ever go to a New Year's party again, I am convinced.

Again this year, as the day approaches (the eve of the day), I find myself looking forward to it with a sense of sad inevitability, holding out some hope that I will find myself in some company that can content itself with merely eating All The Cheese and drinking All The Wine, and will not at the eleventh hour fall prey to a predictable and ill-fated urge to "go do something" for the ringing in of the new year. I fear, with an idle and bland fear, that this is a vain hope.

Attempting to excavate the trash heap of my memory in order to turn up some examples of truly satisfying New Year's Eves, only two out of the three that suggest themselves have to do with food (the odd one out involved spending the night alone with my partner, neither leaving my room, nor turning on the lights). The first, only last year, was unfortunately only a preamble to the eventual mistake of party-hopping, and so is more firmly impressed upon my memory not only because of the warmth of the conversation, bouillabaisse, and Brussels sprouts, but because of how starkly that contrasted with the bustle, chill, and frustration which enveloped me as soon as I left that living room. As this event returns to me as but a peppering of recollections, I won't attempt to reconstruct the whole meal. I remember pestling garlic, cayenne, olive oil, and bread into a rouille that afternoon, thinking hard about maple syrup and bacon as an alternative to butter and white wine for Brussels sprouts, and being very conscious of the birth of my adult appreciation for seafood[1].

Bouillabaisse, who knew?

The second I cannot assign a particular year, but it must have been prior to my entering adolescence and the public sphere of New Year's revelry; some or other New Year's of my childhood, when my parents had some people over (Friends? Family? It remains indistinct), and we all just ate and were merry and I was excited to stay up. The food was "special" in the sense that it was declared so, or made so by the occasion itself (in a satisfying circularity) more than that it was in itself something particularly noteworthy. I remember chili, certainly, some version of Swedish meatballs, and possibly those assorted "Asian" finger-foods that one could get in the freezer section of the local grocery store. There is an age at which the exoticism of an egg roll is not lessened by it being oven-baked, and however much one might balk now at the thought, its passing cannot but be mourned.[2]

If the pattern constituting my wariness re: leaving the Warm Food Place need be further impressed, I could also add the first time I had a wheel of brie stuffed with apricot *confit* and baked in phyllo pastry, then proceeded to leave the house in order to get in a streetcar accident at 11:45pm. I trust I needn't.

So. The clock ticks, the hammer falls. Show me what you got, Toronto.

---

1 See "*Et Tu?*"
2 I believe I also stayed up late watching *Predator* with my brother, and am considering just bringing a copy along to wherever I'm going this year, because in a pinch I'm convinced it could win the day.

Gramaungere

Gramaungere, *noun* a great meal.

Obviously from French in some way (*grand*/big, *manger*/ to eat). Interestingly, Kuhn & Kurath's Middle English Dictionary also supplies its figurative use to denote "an overambitious enterprise." I wonder if that refers to the enterprise of preparing or consuming such a grand meal?

Oh oh oh! But man, *that* gives me (faint, possibly false) insight into this cryptic aside in the OED: *"not from the original FR, which has 'do you think that you can eat up all the pagans by yourself?'"*

Because that would be an overambitious enterprise, no?

The Chip Returns, Part Two:
On the Somethingth Day We Are Risen

Today I mistook for potato chips what turned out, upon more considered scrutiny, to be flower petals strewn upon the metro floor. "Tulip?" I thought to myself. "Gardenia, perhaps?" I am no anthophile. They were yellow, all but one that had an oranging around the edge. It is fleetingly amusing to reflect on the process of realization—the series of swift, internal negotiations with the empirical data that my brain had to make in order to accommodate the reality of the flowers I was seeing to the chips that I was imagining them to be. It went something like this:

"What ho, chips?

"Very bright, very smooth... probably then something like Pringles or some other regurgitated, cookie-cutter chip? That explains their uniform convexity.

"And one, around the edge just a little bit browned, even burned. But damn, they are bright chips. So saturated and vivid their palette.

"Ah. Flower petals. I see."

I know I didn't need to take you through that, and perhaps the scene would have been better left to impress itself gradually upon your mind; the folly of a (modern) man so numbed, blinded to natural beauty, enthralled by fat and salt and the fryer that he mistakes flower petals for potato chips. But as the pages turn and this proves to be the sad central metaphor of my story, the *geschichtegeist* of my biography, I shan't leave myself open to mockery by not remarking the moment as it occurred, even if the meaning, predictably, escapes me.

Or does it? Who am I to submit to the vulgar, romanticist privileging of the flower petal over the potato chip? Am I any less the master of my fate enchanted by the chip—possibly the emblem of Capital and Fast Food, increasing the price of a potato by an order of magnitude by boiling away in oil whatever meager sustenance it once provided-than by the flower? The Flower, itself only brought into my purview by way of centuries of selective breeding and European ecological imperialism, rendered attractive by the insidious machinations of enforced evolution? I feel no more compromised by the chip's salty, "bad fat" appeal to my appetites than the perfumed garishness of the flower.

By this time the metro has carried me deep into the substrate of the city, where no root or tuber finds purchase, but the dep and florist both ply their trade.

> The first time, on our way to Germany, we had sat downstairs while our meal was being made. There were big soft leather chairs, and on the dark table was a bowl of the first potato chips I ever saw in Europe, not the uniformly thin uniformly golden ones that come out of waxed bags here at home, but light and dark, thick and paper-thin, fried in real butter and then salted casually with the *gros sal* served in the country with the *pot-au-feu*.
>
> They were so good that I ate them with the kind of slow sensuous concentration that pregnant women are supposed to feel for chocolate-cake-at-three-in-the-morning. I suppose I should

be ashamed to admit that I drank two or three glasses of red port in the same strange private orgy of enjoyment. It seems impossible, but the fact remains that it was one of the keenest gastronomic moments of my life.

–MFK Fisher, "The Measure of My Powers,"
The Gastronomical Me, 1931-1932

It is problematic to reduce a food to a mere mnemonic device (I do not suggest that this is what Fisher does above), allowing the associated memory to eclipse the very thing that evoked it. Or, if not *problematic* (it is not a problem for everyone, but it is this elision that I seize upon in order to problematize this treatment of memory as easy recall), then disrespectful to the poor food that has done the better part of the work for you.

Madeleine l'Engle has a famous illustration of time travel of an ant traversing a string held between two hands, it assumes that you are the ant, moving from the present to the past. To abuse this metaphor, we might alternately think of it with the food in question as the ant, allowing to be brought together, as the hands, the You of the present and the You of the past. To say, "These chips remind me of the time that we _____" silently disavows that what you mean is, "These chips remind me of the time that we were eating chips and _____." You know, assuming there were chips involved in both instances.

Forgive me if I have traded Swann's garden for the snack aisle, but the chip was here first.

And the chip returns.

I'll Never See Such Arms Again,
In Wrestling or in Love

A few weeks ago I was seized with the compulsion to write a haiku about the strange goings-on in my fridge. Put simply, everything was going bad. I was inclined to attribute it to the massive quantity of expired cheese that we had seen fit to stock it with, leading to a profound upset of the bacterial communities therein. Quite possibly that doesn't make any sense, but weak interest in explanation leads me to embrace (in sort of a one-arm hug, a more comradely over-the-shoulder kind of thing) weak correlation-as-causation. Soups were turning in a matter of days, and ancient, long-relied-upon condiments were blossoming into fantastic moulds and massive ferments overnight.

The poetry seemed uncharacteristic of me, so, having a reputation to maintain, I resisted the urge, fortified by a solid confidence that the results would be at best poor, at worst tacky and insulting to the entire artistic history of Japan.

The cheese was eventually eaten and equilibrium restored, but I am sad to report that it was to be short-lived; for after a long, hard hike, my fridge is dying.

You can imagine I'm upset, but this morning it dawned on me that all frustration aside (all the more frustrating perhaps because it seems to be warming at a clip just out of sync with the falling external temperature, such that it remains just shy of feasible to transfer the remaining contents to the out-of-doors to take advantage of the season's mounting natural refrigeration), perhaps it was more appropriately a time of reflection, a time to look back over the long, obscene partnership the fridge and I have shared...

I remember the first time, five years ago, when a stray foot or broom caught some exposed wiring and the fridge responded by producing a lightning-bright, softball-sized explosion accompanied by an evacuation of some to-this-day-unidentified brown substance from its underbelly. We thought it deceased then as well, and somehow it took us several days before we realized that it had just blown a fuse and that half of our apartment was also powerless. Unbelievably, it took several more such occurrences for us to conclude that perhaps we should tie off the exposed ends of those wires, as opposed to merely routinizing the situation's volatility ("Careful when you're sweeping you don't touch the bottom of the fridge or it'll explode and put out all the lights.").

Or my first Christmas spent in town, when we assembled a clawful of other geographical orphans[1] for the epic production and consumption of a homemade tofurkey (which resembled more than anything half a basketball filled with stuffing, but tasted utterly delicious). I had stowed a two-litre torpedo bottle of cola in the freezer earlier in the day for rum & coke purposes. When I went to retrieve the bottle, it, of course, slipped from my hands and crashed to the floor, bouncing a full foot high before, upon second impact, exploding off its cap and rocketing, propelled by a jet of foaming pop, across twenty metres of carpet to slam into the opposite wall. There it lay, exhausted and spent of its nectar (ew, did I really write that?), but no *sabré champagne* could have so earnestly and fittingly sounded the dinner knell for us-young punks clinging together for warmth against the winter chill.

———

Living in Montréal it is standard for one's apartment to come unequipped with a stove or refrigerator, so of course when we moved down the street and up a narrow, perilously unsound flight of stairs, the fridge came with. And I shall remember forever how in navigating those stairs I felt as close to a poetically just death as I ever have. Desperately trying to get a purchase on the fridge's slick, hansa-yellow

---

1 Montréal is one of those cities often described as a place where "everyone is from somewhere else." Obviously this is less the case if one actually hangs around with francophones, but for many anglo punks and other such layabouts attracted by the cheap rent and European savour, this impression rings true. As punks tend to be of a persuasion that is poor and/or estranged from their families, they accordingly do not often make it home for Christmas, assuming they celebrated it in the first place. For my own part, I have the fondest regard for my family, but since my grandmother who functioned as the nexus of holiday getting-together passed away, my parents did not have so much of an investment in the Christmas rigmarole that they felt it worth getting a new tradition going, especially with my brother and I living out of province. Christmas had never been that big a production in our family anyway, and certainly not a religious one, so I never developed quite the hate-on for it that many people seem to carry around. Thus I was very interested in salvaging some of the more pleasant associations of the holiday and filtering them through the flattering light of voluntary association, in the spirit of building new "family traditions" in a new city. Also, after years of vegan potlucks and squatting on the floor like a bunch of cave people, I had become very keen on the ritual of everyone sitting around an actual common table. And so was initiated the tradition of Orphan Christmas, for which my house was known to host for several years until, ironically, the sheer number of people who were not able or interested in going home and were too legitimately my friends to be excluded grew so large as to render the "one dinner, one table" principle unworkable, and so I gave the whole thing up and became a Zoroastrian.

metal sides in the bathwater humidity of mid-July.

—

Then there were the waves of varying fickleness to which we were subjected—the several months in the summer when we couldn't keep greens of any sort in the fridge for more than twelve hours, lest the fridge see fit to freeze them solid. We eventually worked out a compromise whereby we acquiesced to the fridge's insistence that the bottom shelf and right-most crisper drawer remain at a just above freezer temperature. I cannot help but see this arrangement as a socio-technical *dispositif* integral to the organization of our drinking habits; in the interest of not wasting fridge space, said crisper drawer was rechristened the "Beer Drawer," beer being the only thing that would not immediately freeze.

And what kind of Beer Drawer is not kept well stocked?

A poor one, of course, but what kind of Beer Stock is not subjected to regular turnover?

A poorly-utilized one, and so far be it from us to leave ourselves open to accusations of hoarding! As the saying goes, from each according to their ability, to each according to their need! And we being *able and needy men*, the Beer Drawer was allowed to fulfill its purpose, cheerfully abetted and unmolested.

—

And now, five years along (it's not clear where or whence it even came from in the first place, but it bears a distinctly 1970s aesthetic, so I can only presume it served many families before us), after many times rallying itself on the brink of death (last spring, for example, when for a week it sounded as if its fan was chopping its insides into tattered ribbons. We took to turning it off at night to offer it and us sufficient respite to sleep a night through) it appears that the fridge is losing its tenuous grasp on life. For a while we were fighting a pitched battle—ratcheting up the internal temperature dial, fiddling with the exposed wires underneath-but every time I open it up and put my hand to its side the body grows warmer still. I can no longer pretend that I don't need to acquire a new refrigerator, and with a quickness; that the mourning must be brief.

So I bid it adieu (to the balcony, where it has been sitting for the past six months), not pissed, but wistful.

L'Assassinat de Carala

You find yourself standing in the Dollarama, listening to the *Elevator to the Gallows* soundtrack and puzzling over how *all* the rocks glasses can seemingly be defective in exactly the same way—the inside bottom of the glass is skewed to one side, in every case. Maybe the factory lists to one side?- and you begin to become suspicious that your life is some manner of neo-realist nightmare. This produces equal measures of pleasure and embarrassment, and persists, no thanks to Domino, the Dollarama version of Ferrero Rocher. Five to a pack instead of three, and tasting approximately, but in the final analysis unconvincingly, like their inspiration; they are more dome-like than spherical, the wafer a little more diaphanous, the hazelnut inexplicably more elusive (or maybe just smaller? In the first one I ate I almost missed it entirely), but at least the chocolate is "chocolate" and not merely "chocolatey."

"Chocolatey confection" is perhaps my favourite modern evasion (I was going to say euphemism, but I guess it really isn't a euphemism. It's just the truth), and there is no shortage of it to be found at the Dollarama (as at Dollarama's own fraternal emulation, the One Dollar And More store, which has lost even its own peculiar cachet now that Dollarama stocks $1.25, $1.50, $2.00 items). Tonight, "wafers with chocolatey content" as the package proclaims, kick it up a previously uncarved notch by hedging on whether their "content" provides semantically sufficient grounds to qualify as "filling" (Wafer Exec One: "Well, I don't know that it's really *filling* the space; it's just sort of sitting there." Wafer Exec Two: "I agree, after that 'peanutty' legal debacle, WaferCo can't afford to take another hit").

So back out into the dark, sufficiently unhinged by Black Mischief and Dominos that everything looks and tastes and feels just unreal enough to keep you entertained for the four blocks home, where you will sit with your cat and watch cat videos on the Internet, you pretending you're doing it for her sake, she pretending she can make sense of the images moving before her.

Spice—It's the Spice of Life

There are days that one's opening volley of sustenance, rather than launching one into the day nourished and alert, has the effect of stultifying the faculties and propelling one backward into the torpor and befuddledness of sleep. I have come to recognize that in this, the twilight of my youth, anything approaching a "hearty" breakfast has just this effect. Anything more than a couple of eggs and a small serving of toast presents me immediately with the sensation of thickening about the middle and lowers my centre of gravity just when I most need to be lightest on my feet. Perhaps it is a measure of the life that I live that in the morning it is less important that I am solid and *imbouleversable*[1] than it is that upon being knocked down I am able to nimbly spring back to my feet, alert and primed for *riposte*. I may further attribute this preference for simple breakfasts to the probability

---

1 I was all set to take deserved flack for neologizing in a language that is not even my own, but it turns out that there is precedent for the word. Jean Baptiste Richard de Randonvilliers included it in his 1842 *Enrichissement de la Langue Française*, although it seems not to have made it into "proper" French, staunch prescriptivists that *Académie Française* are. Since the apogee of my facility with French (ironically not a half-decade into residing in Québec, but while in high school French Immersion), the one word that I have continuously yearned to import, for lack of a suitable equivalent, into English, has been *bouleversement*. It strictly means "overturned" or "up-ended," but connotes both discombobulation (a word for which I have never had much fondness) and psychological disturbance, and anyone who has ever had the experience of being swiftly up-ended and enjoyed sufficient time to appreciate the experience of reorientation before crashing into a heap, will share my belief that it deserves a word that so idiophonically suits it. You must admit that it comes off better than "unoverturnable."

that I had eaten late and greatly the night before, and so spent the sleeping hours digesting in lieu of resting. After such a night of travail it is important that I merely stimulate the activity of my stomach, not overload it.

It is in the interest of such stimulation that I recommend the practice of taking spicy for breakfast. I could have written "eating something spicy for breakfast," but that is honestly not how it appears in my mind. Somewhere between the old tradition of "taking a cure" (usually repairing to some European spa, such as the baths at Nîmes, to be treated for alcoholism or uppityness or St. Vitus Dance, or like, infidelity) and a Platonic idea sits "spicy for breakfast," and I can imagine myself saying, as I have myself thought, "Oh yeah, can't go wrong with spicy for breakfast," as if it were already a *thing*, like a thing that people say, which it isn't and they don't. At least not yet.

A couple of years ago I found myself appended to a family camping trip in the Killarney region of northern Ontario that instilled me with profound respect for the superiority of the canoe trip to other forms of wilderness adventure. Not only because it involves so much less accursed walking, but because the burden-bearing being done by the canoes affords one's party so much more leeway where provisioning is concerned. Now I am not one of those deplorable urbanites who would insist upon all the creature comforts to keep the uncomfortable creatures and caprices of the wilderness itself at bay-I know full well there can be no greater repast than a can of baked beans with a slug of whiskey, some hot sauce, and a piece of bread, if eaten in proper surroundings. But not having to eat *everything* out of cans can certainly brighten the culinary landscape of the camper.

But I am getting off topic. The father of the party was

a charming old British man, of the friendly and red-faced, as opposed to the genteel variety. He would speak wistfully of his lesbian ex-wife, become perhaps too strident while discussing the bee crisis, and evince the slightest hint of the doddering when well-corned with scotch. But what I recall most vividly was his habit of breakfasting on tea and toast spread with Patak's curry paste.[2] Now for some reason when I was young I had it in my head that straight Patak's was in some way poisonous, probably as the result of the youth's ability to transform something said casually in passing into a statement of fact. "Woof, straight Patak's will kill you," was probably meant as a comment on the potency of the stuff, not a categorical statement; like how "An adult chimp'll tear the arm off a grown man!" is meant to give an idea of the strength of the animal, not a warning about the deep-seated and biological penchant of chimpanzees for human dismemberment.

But what spicier and more aromatic breakfast could one make but Patak's on toast? I will admit that I have not made a habit of eating this, but it is evoked by a breakfast that has become very dear to my heart, which is margarine,[3] honey, and harissa on toast. This is best with buckwheat honey, that almost molasses-like stuff that so well complements the bitterness and hint of smoke of the harissa. Any honey will do, though I recommend that with a faint medicinal twang over the more processed and luxuriant varieties. I

---

2 Patak's is a popular and widely available brand of pre-made curry pastes for use in... just about whatever. I don't recall whether he favoured a particular style, but they are all quite pungent.

3 I have written elsewhere in defence of margarine (see "When In Doubt, Put Some Gravy On It"), and while I think that butter could well be substituted here, I appreciate the *lack* of richness that margarine imparts. For a more sensual snack, I heartily encourage the use of butter instead.

am a great fan of harissa, and am never without a tube of that humble *Phare du Cap Bon* from Tunisia in my larder. I do not know the orthodoxies of harissa. I have been told that harissa simply means "hot sauce" in Arabic, or at least means "hot sauce" to Arabs of various countries, and so I expect its constitution is regionally quite variable.

What I love about the Tunisian varieties that I've had (as well as one Berbere harissa I tried) is their inclusion of toasted caraway and coriander that give them a common sturdy character quite distinct from the saltier, lemon-laced Moroccan versions that remind me of Portuguese *peri peri* sauces such as Macarico. It is this quality, combined with its lack of pronounced acidity, that makes Tunisian harissa such a suitable means of introducing heat into breakfast for, unlike most hot sauces, it does not clash with one's coffee. In fact, I find there to be a very engaging interplay between harissa and a thick, dark espresso. At home I like my espresso bitter, black, and burly and leave appreciation of citrus and almond notes and the like to the baristas with the know-how and equipment to do it right. So it is the bitter, the nutty, and the roasty elements of the harissa and coffee both that make for such an interesting tussle on the palate, enlivened by the slight acidity of the coffee, on the one hand, and the smoky heat of the harissa on the other. It also goes amazingly well on eggs (fried or poached, more so than scrambled), excepting the honey.

And so, rather than deadening one's faculties with heavier fare before one even gets out the gate, a bit of spicy for breakfast, the ol' honey & harissa on toast (maybe with an egg just to the left), provides one with just enough suste-nance to embark upon the day, while allowing one looking forward to being hungry enough to truly appreciate one's lunch. And we all know that in their proper measure, bitter-ness and spice both serve to stimulate and sensitize not only gorge and gut, but intellect as well.

It's a good life if you don't weaken.

Ingurgitate

Ingurgitate, *verb* **1** to swallow greedily or immoderately (food, or, in later use, esp. drink) to glut or gorge oneself. (fig.) to engulf. (from L. *ingurgitare*—to pour in [like a flood].)

2 to eat or drink to excess; to gormandize, guzzle.

3 to gorge, to cram with food or drink.

also, to swallow up as a gulf or a whirlpool, to engulf.

How is that for rich, eh? What poetic wealth! I don't recall how I came upon *ingurgitate* in the first place; it wasn't via Shea, I just checked, so it must have been through my own boundless (although easily foiled if not immediately satiated, being as just as nature abhors a vacuum, so I a challenge) curiosity. I'm inclined to think it derived from thinking about *regurgitate* and wondering whether the root was otherwise employed, for example, was it possible to *gurgitate* something? Turns out no. Well, technically yes but practically no, insofar as the OED designates it both rare *and* obsolete. Let us assume it is best to leave that stone, if turned, unthrown.

I think I inherited some of this interest in the directionality of word mechanics (I'm sure there's a name for this, linguists) from my father, who was a big fan of calling things "*couth*," and derived great satisfaction from such similarly correct-if-uncommon kinds of wordplay. He is also the man who twice in my life managed to shock me into an appreciation of jam and cheese, independently of my existing awareness that fruits and cheese go perfectly well together, so why not jam and cheese? I'd be more ashamed of not having thought of it before (twice) were it not for the skepticism I am still met with most of the time I bring it up. In fact, just the other week I went into this little *casse-croute* in Verdun and ordered a grilled cheese sandwich and a packet of jam, and, apple emulating the tree whom I had witnessed do just so, spread that shit right on top. It was delicious!

I passed it around and no one could cast any more serious aspersions on the taste than could be accounted for by the fact that it came from a *casse-croute* (hence made with white bread & processed cheese).

So give it a shot, dudes. Jam and cheese.

Anyway, what's up with the letter G? I don't think if you had ever asked would I have imagined that I had a particular fondness for it (I admit I am in a way attracted to it, grudgingly, on the basis of my total inability to render it in lower-case as such: g. I can manage *g*, but g? No way! Can anyone?). And yet there is this whole slew of g-words that I totally love, which seem to coincidentally have to do with some manner of corporeal excess, often, if not specifically *gastronomic* in character: gormandize, gut, glut, gorge, gustatory, gulf, grotesque, glutton, gulchin,[1]—gore, even.

I say *coincidentally* not because it is odd that I love these excessive g-words—it is well established that I am preoccupied with various forms of excess, both conceptual and actual—but because it seems curious that so many of them

---

1 See "Gulchin."

start with g in the first place. It suggests, although does not necessitate, some common etymological origin, and in such a way that it is astonishing that some common set, some common notion could have so (un?)healthily prodigious a get. It's... gargantuan, really.

Brassica Uber Alles, Part Two: Roman Fever Revisited

IT IS THAT TIME OF THE YEAR.

Which is variably, I have noticed, the last two weeks of August or July.

Alternately:

RAPINI TIME.

That hotly anticipated time when—for those of us who don't live in Italian-dominated neighbourhoods, where that shit runs like water—rapini descends from its three-dollar-throne-on-high and suddenly becomes attainable for a buck or two, which is Awesome, and then I end up eating it every day until I have pretty much ruined it for myself, but whatever dude, "this path is stupid, it goes in spirals, perhaps in circles, but whichever way it goes, I will follow it."[1]

And if you need to know what to do with rapini, aka broccoli rabe, broccoli raab, broccoletti (but not *broccolini*), or *cime di rape* (which means "turnip top," because they are both cruciferous vegetables. Beware their crucifury), just do what you should do to every vegetable: cut off the tough, inedible parts (in this case, the basest, woodiest end of the stalk), sauté some onions and tons of garlic in as much butter and olive oil as you can afford to eat in one sitting, then add the vegetable in question (uh, rapini), some salt and pepper, and braise till done in a white wine that is otherwise good enough to drink. You can cover it for a bit if you

---

1 *Siddhartha*, Hermann Hesse (1922)

120

want, but you gotta time it so that the wine still cooks down sufficiently to form a sauce with the butter and olive oil, of which I usually add more at the end. And a squirt of lemon, but only at the end.

I was hoping to unearth some rich folkloric history for rapini, but it doesn't appear to have been a major player, mythologically. In lieu, however, I can offer personal anecdote, ie: the stuff of future myth.

On the cusp of the winter of 2009, I found myself in Rome for the second time in as many years, after more than two decades of abject Romelessness (I might even say that I was happily Romeless, having no idea what I was missing, save that there was perhaps a wolf involved, some alliteratively-named dog-children, the apex and decline of a great empire, and the decline of Morrissey's songwriting into sentimentality and affected bitterness). Still quite conscious of Rome as the home of The Best Piece of Pizza I'd Ever Had[2] I resolved to find again the little side street market that so impressed me the first time around.

As I became increasingly confident in the odds (however unlikely) of finding this establishment (I knew it was on the other side from an epic fort of an epic bridge; a real fort-storming bridge), I began to feel a mounting anxiety—for I am all too conscious of the perverse flim-flammery of memory; certainly I had much benefitted from having this singular pizza experience, but what mythologizing had my mind already undertaken? How could I reasonably expect, should I find it again, this pizza to bear the weight of the mantle that I had bestowed upon it in recollection? Wouldn't even the most craftsmanly of crusts deteriorate

---

2 See "In Which Two Edith Wharton Characters Admit To Mutual and Increasingly Shattering Betrayals."

under so romantic a burden?

This is how I live. Can you believe it?

So over what I am pretty certain was the Ponte Sant'Angelo, and onto the side street that emerged out of my hazy brain into the cold, prohibitive light of geographical reality; where in moments I was standing, closely surrounded on all sides by the same (well, probably different) walls of pasta, olive oil, and pizza of my memory.

And as luck would have it, they didn't have the pizza I had before. The fresh basil/green tomato/*mozzarella di bufala*? Nope. Good. I got the rapini and sausage, and it was awesome.

—

I dare say it may have been The *Second Best Piece of Pizza I've Ever Had* (and I've had a lot of pizza).

So thanks, rapini. Thanks for saving me, you know, *from myself.*

Bottled Symbolic/Semantic Violence

In search of a good Fancy Cocktail Bar, I and a friend ended up at L'Assommoir in the ol' Vieux-Port, the results of which experience were a) expensive, and b) somewhat disappointing, if still instructive.

Now maybe I just don't know good cocktails, or perhaps as a borderline bibber I prefer mine stiffer than is reasonably to be expected in polite company, but there was definitely something of a middling quality to most of what we each had. They being *Manhattan, Ginger'tini, Espresso Martini*, and *Sazerac, Dry Martini, American Beauty*, respectively.

The bar itself was sufficiently classy[1] to serve as backdrop for our intended masquerade as *nouveaux riches*, and on a not Friday night it might be actively pleasant to be in, but the combination of the bumpin' (shudder) atmosphere and only-decent cocktails made for some underwhelming shit. It's a good thing we two are so charming and attractive, otherwise the night may have been lost!

So, on the topic of the stuff of the thing:

---

1 i.e. Costly. It is important here to distinguish between the two kinds of classy. There's "ooh, *classy*," which means expensive and a bit horrid, populated by men who gel their hair and if they wear ties have never buttoned the top button in their *lives*, and there is "you know, this is a pretty classy joint," which means that there's a quiet dignity that pervades the space, however raucous the atmosphere may become, and the staff are either painfully professional or genuinely charming, and maybe even professionally charming, but at least genuinely professionally charming. No *mauvaise foi* here. And if you're wondering, no, I haven't ever been to the latter place, and probably it doesn't exist, outside of the memoirs of the Left Bank.

THE MANHATTAN – Too sweet. Not burly enough, in either of our opinions. What I like about Manhattans is, like a lot of classic cocktails, it's booze cut with booze (in which case it's rather less like 'cutting' and more akin to He-Man and Skeletor combining their two Power Swords to make the One True Power Sword, which is AWESOME (if I remember correctly)) so it has that effect of making a Good Idea Better/Bad Idea Worse, so when you get a weak Manhattan you get to wondering what they put in to somehow make it less boozy than either of the primary ingredients. But they did ask whether my compatriot wanted it in a rocks or martini glass. I like that.

THE GINGER'TINI – I don't know why that requires an apostrophe, whereas the Chocolatini does not. I mean, every _____-*tini* is going to be a bit of a wash because you're mussing about with the simplicity of a drink which is also, and at its best just barely, booze cut with other booze, and while the slice of ginger garnish was a nice touch, we found it neither boozy nor gingery enough.

THE ESPRESSO MARTINI – I can't be more specific about this, but it just seemed like a weak Black Russian, with supposedly a shot of espresso in it, which you know, should have been great, but it just kinda mehhed. One begins to suspect we are undertasters?

THE SAZERAC – This was actually delicious, but I kick myself for not paying attention when they were making it, so I didn't see whether they used actual Peychaud's bitters (which as far as I can tell you can't get in Québec, which... maybe also means you are not allowed to sell/use commercially in Québec?), or what kind of Absinthe—as it's not even listed as an ingredient on the menu, but the barman did make a point of mentioning its inclusion when serving me—so who knows what's really in it. He did do something involving a lemon peel catching fire, though, which I appreciated, because I am a child/Magic Lover/flying insect.

THE MARTINI – Gin (obviously), dry, one olive—I will admit that I am still pretty new to martinis, but I love gin so maybe I should have asked for extra dry, because again, not so much kick.

THE AMERICAN BEAUTY – Sounded great, sounded fancy (cognac, port, OJ and strawberry *coulis*), and honestly I appreciated that you really could taste the cognac, but it wasn't something that felt... *made*, so much as it did a glass in which multiple different things were put. You know? It didn't achieve that almost alchemical *gestalt* that some cocktails carry around in their hidden heart. It's a shame, that.

And another thing, a point of some contention, sure, but a good cocktail shouldn't come across as if it's trying to mask the taste of the alcohol, in my opinion. It, like all foods involving multiple ingredients, should be about putting the component parts into a productive interplay, that allows you to appreciate in a different fashion (in a different light, if you will, e.g. the light of vermouth) the flavours of the alcohol. This is ideally speaking, obviously. Historically, while Prohibition was one of the cocktail's heydays, it probably contributed mightily to the former phenomenon, because in all likelihood you can do without a more nuanced appreciation of bathtub gin.

And that's alls I know.

Actually, you want to know what else has been getting to me? The name. The name of the damn place. *L'Assommoir*, I have discovered, is the name of a novel by Emile Zola dealing with the ravages of alcoholism amongst the impoverished Parisian working class. *Oh, ha ha ha*, what more delicious irony could there be for we, the rich and literate, enjoying *nos martinis funkys* and our third *ceviche* at so-named a bar! It just seems a little *gauche*, no?

Outside of the specifically literary and political connotations, what really gets on my nerves (predictably) is that *un assommoir* is an old colloquial term for a little booze shop that sells (usually) its own liquor of... dubious quality, or as the *Larousse* puts it, *"les boissons de dernière catégorie"* and what is adorable about that bit of idiom is that it derives from the verb *assomer*, which means to throttle, bludgeon, or otherwise render senseless, thus making it a great little name for a bar, but one where six drinks tab up to eighty dollars, and there is not even an affectation Hard Times? No thanks.

But I don't mean for it to sound like a horrible time. I enjoyed every moment of it, and I am not convinced that they are bad at making cocktails (I mean, they have made their name with it), but rather that until I find a bar with an ambience to my tastes, I'd rather just make 'em at home, and eat my own olives while I'm at it.

Ultimately, I can appreciate the poetic justice that in dissimulating *nouveau riche* we just nudged ourselves that little bit further into that gutter of insolvency in and about which we cavort and gambol so happily (if not carelessly).

Joke's on us?

Taps is Just Reveille for the Hidden Kingdom

or
You're my Princess Toadstool

Hopefully, because they are delicious, you are all familiar with *trompettes de la mort*—a smallish, greyish mushroom resembling the chanterelle in appearance, if not lineage or necessarily taste (I find the *trompette* not quite as exciting, a little earthier, nuttier, less delicate), hence their occasional (mis)representation as *black chanterelles*. I dare say *mis* because they really are not chanterelles, and belong to a different genus entirely—*craterellus cornucopioides* v. *cantherellus cibarius*, respectively—small potatoes perhaps, the hairs upon them split, but why taxonomy at all, if not for quibbling distinctions such as these?

Far more interesting to me, however, are the variety of other names the mushroom enjoys. Somewhat to my chagrin I realize that I have been calling them *trompettes de mort* up until now, which falls, slightly less grammatically correct, between *trompettes de la mort* (trumpets of death) and *trompettes des morts* (trumpets of the dead). This is a distinction which I find poetically, if not practically, significant—perhaps contemplating whether they are the trumpets heralding the dead or those blown *by* the dead (To herald themselves? To party?) is a pleasurable component of the culinary experience only for assholes like me?

These mushrooms are also called *cornes d'abondance*

(horns of plenty), ironically, this dual naming seeming to suggest a sort of "just think of the bounty that flows forth from death's cup" exhortation. But while they don't (unlike other, less morbidly-identified fungi) actually kill you, it occurs to me just this very moment that the seemingly opposed nomenclature actually says just that—something very *apposite* about mushrooms in general, the saprophytic (death-eating)[1] ones at least: that great bounty does, in the form of delicious fruiting bodies and soil/partner-plant-nourishing mycorrhizae, derive from the dead and decaying and decayed. How exciting!

But Then You Had To Go And Bring Race Into It, Didn't You?

Because it all started with this note from a friend:

---

[1] While writing this it struck me that I didn't know exactly how widely the designation *saprophyte* applied. I mean, if saprophytes are merely eaters of death, then would not all carnivores and many herbivores (herbivores being slightly more likely to consume their food while it is still "alive") be *saprophytes*? Or, more correctly, *saprophages*?

sapro*phyte* – organism, usually plant or fungus, that survives off dead or decaying organic matter.

sapro*phage* – organism which "eats" dead or decaying matter.

sapro*troph* – organism which derives its nutrients from dead or decaying matter (a saprotroph is thus a kind of *heterotroph*, which must derive its nutrients from other sources, as opposed to *autotrophs*, which can manufacture their own nutritional requirements chemically, from the sun and soil. like you know, most plants.)

So then I'm thinking maybe it's specifically *decaying* (not merely dead) matter? But as far as the numerous not very detailed definitions can tell me, no, it's not *specifically* decaying matter. My suspicion, which has yet to be validated, is that it is intended to refer, or refers *de facto*, if not *de jure*, to organisms which derive their nutrition from dead organic matter by secreting some sort of digestive enzyme or something into the material and then reabsorbing components of the matter, thus participating in its decomposition. This seems scientifically sloppy, but it's the closest I can get to a designation that makes sense.

Oh, and re: mushrooms, I saw Trompettes de Mort on a deli menu here in York, but they'd changed it to Trompettes de Maures, which means (I just looked this up) MOORS.

Which indeed it does! And what up with this? Well, no one really seems to know, but the general consensus is that it is probably a combination of typo (it is a homophone, after all) and marketing ploy, because the wary restaurant-goer might be propelled into outright *caginess* confronted by an unfamiliar death-designated mushroom on a menu (alliteration intentional). Or so Les Coureurs des Bois[2] suggest, and I on my part believe, because they say it so well: *"dans le but d'adoucir son nom rebutant"* ("with the aim of softening their off-putting or repugnant name").

Although forgive me if I at first glance find the association of black mushrooms with black *people* faintly more hackle-raising than the merely macabre, but I am a bit of a PC metalhead (thus more pro-death/anti-racial insensitivity). In fairness to *les trompettes des maures*, however, there is such a thing as a Moorish trumpet, called an *agnafile* or *añafil*, and it bears still more resemblance to the mushroom in question than does a "regular" Western trumpet! (I just found this out! Put that in my pipe and smoke it!)

Postscript: I could not help but think while writing this piece (indeed, all too often when I heard the word *"Moor"*) of the opening lines of Virginia Woolf's *Orlando*:

> He-for there could be no doubt of his sex, though
> the fashion of the time did something to disguise

---

2 Gérald and Ariane, a father-daughter team of foragers who have a show on Québecois television. The original *coureurs des bois* ("runner of the woods") were renegade seventeenth century French-Canadian woodsmen, hunting, trapping, trading without the permission of Colonial authorities.

it—was in the act of slicing at the head of a Moor which swung from the rafters. It was the color of an old football, and more or less the shape of one, save for the sunken cheeks and a strand or two of coarse, dry hair, like the hair on a coconut. Orlando's father, or perhaps his grandfather, had struck it from the shoulders of a vast Pagan who had started up under the moon in the barbarian fields of Africa; and now it swung, gently, perpetually, in the breeze which never ceased blowing through the attic rooms of the gigantic house of the lord who had slain him.

Which, for the movie were exchanged for a scene of young Orlando writing poetry under a tree in the idyllic English countryside. How's *that* for *l'adoucement de la rebutant*? (not to mention a pretty significant change of mise-en-scene for a book/movie all about gender dis/ambiguity and transition...)

Mr. Ben Franklin on How We Live

Highlights from the compendium of contemporary (late 1700s) idioms for drinking submitted by Ben Franklin to the Pennsylvania Gazette, under the pseudonym Mrs. Silence Dogwood.

- Fox'd
- Been to France
- Groatable
- Confoundedly Cut
- Clips the King's English
- Contending with pharaoh
- The malt is above the water
- Been too free with the creature
- Had a thump over the head with Sampson's jawbone

and of course,

- Got on his little hat.

The Cup that Cheers Itself

A.J. Liebling (1904-1963) seems like an awesome guy. He was a prodigious writer, eater of food, and lover of boxing and horse races. He studied French literature at the Sorbonne, a choice that was by his own admission mostly a pretext for eating shit-tons of French food, and went to war for *The New Yorker* (writing, not fighting) off and on between '39 and '44.

After a long and committed (after a fashion) search, I've at last acquired a copy of *Between Meals*, which contains the bulk of his food writing, and at the risk of being plunged into murderous dissatisfaction at the disparity between 1930s Parisian and early twenty-first century Island cuisine, I intend to read it on my upcoming "vacation" in PEI (here's fingers crossed for smoother sailing this time around[1]).

Liebling's *Between Meals* is more or less a memoir of his time in Paris, organized (as the title suggests) around eating, but I have found that some of his most interesting writing on food appears in brief flashes elsewhere. In his attention to what kinds of lunches are provided at the camp of this heavyweight-in-training, or his reception by an aging French colonel in the early stages of the war:

> A soldier wheeled over a tea wagon holding
> about 20 bottles—scotch, port, sherry, and

---

1 See "When There's No One to Blame But Yourself."

132

various apéritifs. The Colonel took an obvious pride in his gamut of alcohols; it proved he could "defend himself". The verb *"se défendre"* had acquired a very broad meaning in the French Army; it signified "getting along"... soldiers going on patrol in wooded parts of no-man's land set rabbit snares so that they might pick up a tasty breakfast—all these expedients were part of the French concept of self defense. It followed logically that a colonel defended himself on a grander scale than a subordinate.

-"Merry Christmas, Horrid New Year," in *The Road Back To Paris*, 1944.

This idea of "self-defence" is totally fascinating to me. On an immediate level, it resonates with the idea of larding oneself against the winter with preserves, ferments, salt cures, grain stores, etc.; basic survival practices in any country beset by seasons.

As a city dweller I find I do this myself in a similar, if less urgent, capacity. When in good financial straits I buy big bags of rice and lentils and jugs of olive oil and the like, as well as, on perhaps an arguably less subsistence level, bottles of brandy and scotch and vermouth for those harder, darker times when funds are stretched and I'm burning my own waste to stay warm. In this way and only in this way am I like Aesop's ant, working now in order to sing the winter away. Or more accurately I spend now so as to eat later without being able necessarily to, say, pay the hydro bill, and so am like some happy, if horrifying, ant/grasshopper hybrid. Can you even imagine? I'm hideous!

Food is also regularly caught up in nationalist discourses,

not only in debates about cultural authenticity, but in the sense of "if we give up these practices that we feel define us, The Enemy wins." This can manifest in more grotesque and less grotesque fashions. The whole "freedom fries" affair was entertaining largely because of how gorily it displayed the capacity of much of good ol' God-bless'd America to be utterly oblivious when it really should be embarrassed by its own stupidity (Lesser attention was garnered by the simultaneous neologism "freedom toast," which I assume is due to Americans' general preference for Action Pancakes). On the other hand, there is something just shy of admirable about it, in that smoking-in-a-swimming-pool sort of way.

There are other such moments in *The Road Back To Paris*, such as when Liebling marvels with a mix of admiration and pity at the French citizenry who try as much as possible to go about their *apéritif* and *éclair* filled lives in concerted indifference to the rapid approach of the front. MFK Fisher, too, explores the delicacy of the balance in her *How To Cook A Wolf*, a book about the strategies of eating well/getting by under wartime shortages and ration cards. Although the message she leaves us with is less that decadence be obstinately insisted upon in the face of mean circumstances than that the lessons of learning to live well with less must not with cannons fade, "*there can be no more shameful carelessness than with the food we eat for life itself.*"

Anyway, returning to the frivolous, or at least to the sometimes desperate necessity of the capacity for frivolity, I'd like to propose a toast: *à nos défenses!*

(Actually, I'd like to propose that we all start *using* this toast, and cheersing thusly.)

—

I have spent a good bit of time dicking around, talking to francophones, trying to sort out the proper reflexive and/ or imperative forms that this might otherwise take, as in, "to our self-defence/to our defence of ourselves" ("*À nous défendrons*"? I still welcome help from any francophones whom I have not yet badgered apropos of this), but in the end I think "*à nos défenses!*" says it approximately as well in its simplicity. And I like how in its apparent simplicity (oh, here it comes), in the act of cheersing, it actually smuggles in a certain reflexivity. As you raise the glass you are saying "let us raise a glass, in cheers, to our defenses—the things that help us get through the everyday struggle—of which there may be many, but in this case is alcohol," and thus you are cheersing with that which you are *cheersing to*, creating a neat little, uh, feedback loop or something. Not unlike, "To alcohol, the cause of, and solution to, all of life's problems," but with a little more panache. Or, tongue less firmly in cheek, like saying, "to *getting by*, and our many ways (this one in particular) of doing so!" and still further: "to us, and our being so good at self-defence, right?"

Right?

I have a predilection for such linguistic (er... conceptual?) contortions—they feel like one of those calming Love Tunnel carnival boat rides (in that they're slow/involve a gradual progression, not because you maybe get to touch a boob) that at some point you realize is actually a (similarly slow) roller coaster riding on a Möbius strip in the inner/ outer space that is meaning ... I do not, contrastingly, have a predilection for M.C. Escher posters. Or getting high.

It reminds me a bit of Nabokov's short story "The Vane Sisters" that I just read wherein the narrator is loosely involved with a couple of loony and ill-fit-for-this-world sisters, one of whom commits suicide while the other dies of something or other, after which the narrator, under the influence of the latter's obsession with symbology and numerology and spiritual hoozlewazzle, skeptically searches for some indication of their spectral presence, only to resign, deflated, and (if not a little smugly) defeated in a final paragraph that acrostically reintroduces the sisters into his textual reality; of which Nabokov writes (a little embarrassedly, I think), "This particular trick can be tried once in a thousand years of fiction. Whether it has come off is another question."[2]

⸻

And, uh...
Let us be that cup.

---

2 It also reminds me of some stuff I wrote about Vikings (see "Quaff While Thou Canst"

I Can't Believe I'm Going to Say This… But Yes, "My Cross to *Beurre*." There, it's Done. Let Us Never Speak of This Again

1. A good croissant is a special thing. A really special thing, in fact, of an order many of us have been conditioned to overlook because we simply have never had one. There are terrible croissants everywhere, *everywhere*, and it feels as with all things that once had a transcendent quality and are increasingly banalized by their subordination to Fordism that they are part of some conspiracy to make us incapable of truly loving this or that food, this or that experience.

It's like outside agitators, planted by the state to destroy The Movement, or like college hippies ruining everything (when hippies were actually kind of touching and charming) or like some terrifying *Captain Planet*-esque corporate villain putting up giant matte paintings of uninspiring sunsets just over every horizon in order to make us hate sunsets.

This is what a bad croissant is like. Or a bad cup of coffee.

But then you have one of those cups of coffee that reminds you that coffee isn't just ground-up monkey shit, it's some kind of fruit or berry or spice that has turned nations on their heads and done perhaps as much for literature as has booze. It is black as pitch or brown as perfect toast and bitter, delicate, a warm embrace and a honing steel, tasting more like licorice or liquor than you ever remembered or could have expected.

And a good croissant is a magic trick, or something like

a temporary success of alchemy—butter into gold/golden crust. My cabinetmaker friend the other day said of it that it is not like a kind of bread that has a lot of butter in it but like butter that has just enough flour in it, and I can't agree more. It is butter, with the light touch of flour coaxing it through the exercise, holding its breath just long enough to convince one that it is a bread. It feels like a temporary structure, waiting to be torn apart by hand, to shatter into flake and panes, and seems as one bites into it to be a suspended liquid somehow not wet. You suspect that somewhere along the line you were recruited into the deception, and it is upon you that it depends—the suspension of disbelief that makes fine patisserie possible.

Like Baron Munchausen raising himself and horse Bucephalus out of the sea by his own ponytail.

A friend suggested, concerned as I am with finding reliable sites of good croissants in this city, that I make a whole project of it—map it out, do some thorough research on the history of the croissant and its many technical foibles—lord knows it is rich enough material, from the debunking of the myth of its crescent-moon shape's origin (commemorating the victory of the French over who, the Turks? Some or other Muslim invader? Bosh, mostly.), to the quiet ritualism of folding and turning and flattening common to all puff pastries... but I don't think I shall. I think instead you get this essay.

Note that I employ only affective and mystical language throughout, successfully (I think) avoiding mobilizing the problematic discourse of authenticity, however sinisterly it lurks in the wings...

2. Getting in a little over my head—while looking for some

etymologically-inflected pun with which to title this post, I ran across some interesting homophonic material related to the croissant. *Croissant*, obviously, is just French for crescent, but it just as obviously does not end (or rather, begin) there. If you are not at all familiar with French conjugation, this will be even less interesting to you, but a rudimentary knowledge of suffixes should, ah, suffice. *Croissant*, as an adjective, means growing, or burgeoning (from the Latin *crescere*). I love how the Oxford-Hachette dictionary frames it—as in *talent, love, industry, crime*. Anyway, this is where we get the croissant, effectively—the shape of the pastry resembles the crescent moon, which is a *waxing* moon.

The infinitive of the verb to grow, or burgeon, in this sense, is *croître*, and when I saw this I was immediately struck by its similarities to both the verbs *croiser* (to cross) and *croire* (to believe). In fact, the first-person-singular of *croître* is *je croîs* (I grow), which is almost audibly indistinguishable from *je crois* (I believe), and I have just learned that, while nigh-imperceptibly lengthening the vowel sound, the *circonflexe* (little hat) mostly serves to mark vowels which used to be followed by an *s* (obviously not the case here, because the s remains), or to distinguish between homographs (words spelled the same). Now this is where I get in a little over my head, because I don't have it in me to figure out when and where and why *croître* picked up its *circonflexe*, but I am struck by how *croîs* and *crois* also sound like *croix* (cross, as in "The Cross," religiously interchangeable, as in English, with crucifix).

> so, croise ? croîs ? crois ? croix,
> (to) cross ? grow ? believe ? (the) Cross.
> croissant ? croissance ? croyance
> crescent ? growth ? belief.

Neat.

Interesting coincidence too, this weird link between the cross and the crescent, respectively emblematic of the two world religions most perpetually in historical conflict.

Now if I was a real linguist or historian or whatever I'd be able to tell you whether that means anything (is it accidental that growth and belief and the cross all share these features? Is it meaningful? We know also that cross comes from the Latin *crux*, and thus not necessarily from *crescare*), but I really am not so I really can't, but it is this very lack of rigour that I think renders my company tolerable. Who really wants to suffer the smug self-satisfaction of the expert, when one could enjoy the fumbling charm of the amateur? But for all my insistence upon *quality* (this is effectively an offshoot of a product review, for god's sake), if there's one lesson to be drawn from my dumb life it's that if you're not going to do something *right*, you should at least enjoy doing it.

Booya.

Part Three: Beyond Taste

Against Brunch

"Hardened Nightbirds Fondly Cherish All Its Subtle Charms"

I don't like brunch.

You can save your sharp intakes of breath, brunch-lovers, because however much this offends your brunch-loving sensibilities, it is but a statement of preference. I do not hate you for what you do, and it is only slightly down my nose that I look at your late-morning/early-afternoon dining activities; one could even argue, as it will be demonstrated, that I may simply suffer from a case of sour grapes.

Where to begin? It is only fair to start with brunch itself, as it emerges onto the historical stage, and work up to my own engagement therewith. "Brunch" enters the OED in the supplement to the 1971 edition, which puts the birth of the word in 1900, although popular accounts trace it to Guy Beringer in a rag called Hunter's Weekly:

> Instead of England's early Sunday dinner, a post-church ordeal of heavy meats and savory pies, why not a new meal, served around noon, that starts with tea or coffee, marmalade and other breakfast fixtures before moving along to the heavier fare? By eliminating the need to get up early on Sunday, brunch would make life brighter for Saturday-

night carousers. It would promote human happiness in other ways as well. Brunch is cheerful, sociable and inciting. It is talk-compelling. It puts you in a good temper, it makes you satisfied with yourself and your fellow beings, it sweeps away the worries and cobwebs of the week.

–"Brunch: A Plea" (1896)

Put thusly, I would have to be hard-hearted and hopelessly contrary to speak ill of brunch, but it is less the idea of the thing than the way it has been institutionalized that chafes me. If one of the functions of brunch is to spare the fast-living the hardships of the usual breakfast/lunch rigmarole, as indeed many have suggested to me, arguing that preparing one's own food is the last thing they wish to contend with upon awaking into a hangover, I counter that the last place I want to be in the early hours of my day is standing in a lineup with a bunch of yahoos, or still worse, surrounded by a hundred or so of such yahoos (and probably a couple of *babies* as well. Babies!) amidst the uniquely brunchy din of scraping chairs and clattering dishware. Oy.

Further, and I don't mean to flatter myself, I have yet to experience an omelette in a restaurant (inevitably nine-dollar-plus) that surpasses one I could make for myself in approximately ninety-nine seconds at home, and I don't expect that when I do, it will be found at "brunch." This has as much to do with the qualities inherent in the omelette itself as with the exigencies of running a brunch setup. The power and the glory of an omelette, in my estimation, reside in the ability to eat it mere moments after it has been slid from pan to plate, only so many moments as are required to for the residual heat to finish cooking the inte-

rior to silky but fragile perfection. If I am in the mood for
something spongy, browned, and sweating, I will take it as
a tortilla with maybe some olives, half drunk off a two-euro
Spanish red, or alternately in a bathroom stall of an Ibizan
nightclub, thank you very much.

But I am not one for big breakfasts these days. This is an
admission which usually allows the brunch-lover to mitigate
the psychological distress caused by my public brunch-dissi-
dence, by separating my argument into What Is Wrong With
Brunch on the one hand, and What Is Wrong With Me on the
other, for it seems to be evidence of some frailty of spirit to be
avowedly "into" food, but not at all times a hopeless glutton.
Most days I would be not only contented with, but elated by
a good croissant and an espresso, or, if I am feeling concerned
about continuing to live, a couple of fried eggs (or the above
described light, "French" omelette) and a piece of toast.

Time was, I couldn't get through the day without a mess
of fried tofu or beans (I continue to be a fan of maple beans),
some rice or quinoa, sweet potato mash, toast, and some kind
of stewed or steamed green; but those were different, and if
you couldn't infer from the menu, vegan, days, and I no longer
require such hearty fare to launch myself into the world.

With some exceptions (and it is here that I think to myself,
as I have been doing increasingly of late, that I am becoming
such a goddamn nominalist that I am bound to make someone sick, one of these days). For it is specifically "brunch"
with its modern trappings that I disdain; I am all for putting
off breakfasting (or for that matter, rising) until midday, I
love a good *portmanteau*, and I appreciate the convivial
atmosphere; gathering, bright- or bleary-eyed, tails bushy or
between one's legs, to face the dawning, mocking, day in fine
company. What I loathe is putting all these things together

only to be met by some abominably restricted menu[1] that forces me to eat honeydew and refuses me spaghetti. I may prefer a light breakfast as far as proper breakfasting goes, but where breaking the fast is concerned, I am happy as a clam to take lunch, even dinner, or hell, clams, for the purpose. Indeed, I'd rather lunch for breakfast than brunch, any day.

I could perhaps trace this dislike of brunch back to my adolescent years of principled/practical miserliness, an outright antagonism toward restaurants, and the veganism that reduced every brunch menu to plain toast or fried potatoes. I certainly shut myself out at an early age from the social pleasures of brunch that many folks have by now had many years to fashion into a emotional investment in brunch as a ritual; so, sour grapes? Maybe. I recall as a child going to a hotel brunch with my father, brother, and grandmother and being astonished to enter this enchanted, improbable realm where one was permitted to have, in abundance, waffles covered in syrupy strawberries, chocolate, and whipped cream without having to consume even a single vegetable by way of gaining entry, but I don't think that I ever had the presence of mind to catalogue that as a first experience of "brunch," as opposed to "buffet" and those excesses it inevitably encourages.

I am not saying "Do not invite me to brunch," but if you would do me the kindness of suggesting a late breakfast or early lunch in its stead, I promise to do my best to suppress whatever frown or disapproving curl of the lip is awakened by the brunch menu that likely ends up greeting us, and content myself with my Bloody Caesar and soft-boiled egg, if only they will be so obliging.

(I may also try to smuggle in a grapefruit. Would that weird you out?)

---

1 I am not opposed to limited, time-of-day-specific menus, *tables-d'hôte*, in general; this is brunch we're talking about.

Ingustable

Ingustable, *adjective* alternately "not fit to be tasted" and "incapable of being tasted; not perceptible by the sense of taste."

That's an interesting little double meaning, I think, because it comes close to being a word which in its polysemy contains its own opposite. Not quite, but close, because "not fit to be tasted" may mean it tastes *so* bad that it is not even worth putting in one's mouth. Tasting very intensely of badness, of course, is not at all like having no taste at all. People could get so confused!

For example: you're at a party and someone's like, "Hey, how's that artichoke dip?" and you say, "Ingustable!" That leaves them being like, "Wait, did he mean inedibly bad, or was that a sarcastic exaggeration of how lacking in flavour it is?"

Who wants to put people in that kind of situation? Geez. If you wanted to be more specific, you could say that it was "disgustingly ingustable," but then everyone would hate you.

One could argue that something that is not finished being seasoned is ingustable because it is not yet ready to be tasted, but I don't think that's how the word is used.

I mean, was used. Which was probably never.

Except in 1646, by Browne: "the body of that element is ingustable, void of all sapidity."

Sapidity, btw, just means taste—the having of taste. Oh,

oh, wait, it also means (like, presumably, gustable) having pleasant taste, ah ha!

I was hoping to find that vapid was somehow related, but I think it may be coincidental. While it *can* mean, "lacking or having lost life, sharpness, or flavor; insipid; flat. as in: *vapid tea*", I don't think rhyming holds a lot of weight, etymologically. Admittedly they are not *un*related: vapid can be traced back to vapour, sapid to the Latin *sapere*, to taste, and we know (now) that aroma and taste are inextricably linked, in terms of the interactions between volatile particulate matter and our sensory reception, but I don't know that it's in any way constitutive of a relation of the sort we're talking about.

Cradled in the Waves, a Little
Bloated, a Little Tempest Toss'd

Field notes from one among many increasingly under-whelming Prodigal returns, with the author's glosses.

August 1ˢᵗ: started strong, delved well into the mysterious mimetic wellspring that is DORITOS ALL NIGHTER CHEESEBURGER CHIPS (also, to a lesser extent, LAST CALL JALAPEÑO POPPERS, which are pretty credibly jalapeñé, but with an admirable 10(ish) different kinds of cheese/milk ingredients). Also LAYS BBQ RIB chips, which are a whopping letdown in contrast to the organoleptirepresentational power of the Doritos. I believe "somebody should send these guys to Doritos School" was uttered at some point.

Anyway, have you *had* these things (the Doritos)? It's insane. And I don't even like Doritos. In fact, there was a time when I could say honestly that of all the foods you could put in front of me (euhhh, within reason?), possibly the only thing that I would not eat just out of sheer compulsion was Doritos (it turns out Sun Chips are in there too—am I like, the only person who realizes that Sun Chips and Smart Food are *awful?*). Anyway, all that has changed with the latest abomination-cum-breakthrough that is ALL NIGHTER CHEESEBURGER.[1]

---

1 You know, not once, but twice have people tried to correct me on the name of these things ("All Nighter" v. "All Night"), and tail-between-my-legs-in-deference-to-my-willingness-to-believe-that-others'-brains-are-not-so-moth-eaten-as-my-own, I usually take it. Turns out, however, that I was right all along! *All Nighter* it is!

Because they are delicious.

Because they taste exactly like a cheeseburger. A cheap, shitty, fast food cheeseburger. It's...astonishing, but it's all there, to an unsettling degree. You can taste the pickles and the mustard and the ketchup and even the goddamn semi-solid-diced-onions-in-onion-matrix that is so characteristic of just that quality of burger. Oh yeah, and burger and processed cheese, those tastes are there too. It's effed up. Unsettlingly like the scifi vision of space food pills that replicate the taste of an entire meal in a single capsule, although why we've got this but I'm still waiting for my hovercar, I have no idea (we can only hope that hover-class license requirements will be sufficiently stringent that nitwits like myself are never able to get behind the wheel, or who knows what fresh hell will rain down from the violated skies). Apparently in "Doritos Late Night Bad Idea" series (of which ALL NIGHTER CHEESEBURGER and LAST CALL JALAPEÑO POPPER are a part) there is also a TACOS AT MIDNIGHT flavour which I've heard is not awful, but sort of disgraceful in its mere adequacy, given that even in its most basic form, the Dorito already consists of about half of the ingredients of your average taco (corn tortilla, cheese).

I'm hoping they pursue this line to its logical extreme, i.e. SHAWARMA ON THE CAN, or for the Montréal market, WAKING UP WITH A HALF-CHEWED MOUTHFUL OF POUTINE.

Also, one normal, one large guru each? What are we thinking? "We'll keep good time on a journey through the past."

Surprisingly, at scenic rest stop X, my almond butter/ chicory/fried egg/tofu pup/Armenian string cheese sandwich is holding up pretty good, if a little condiment sodden (I'm always wary of putting mayonnaise on something that is going to spend more than five hours in a car in the summertime, but it is a risk, I have decided, that is worth taking.

———

7:52pm, New Brunswick Time: we are approached on exiting the IRVING BIG STOP by a middle-aged black woman, "Say excuse me, I heard you boys talking about energy drinks, and you know that those are full of bad stuff for you. Now I want you to take this card, and go to this website, where you'll find some sources of energy that are all natural and good for you."

See: business card (max GXL "the guanine activator", and max N Fuze, with nano activators)

We momentarily were torn by the impulse to point out that we exclusively drank GURU, which is caffeine free, organic and just full of ASIAN MAGIC ROOTS, and VITAMIN WATER, which is full of FOOD COLOURING, MOONBEAMS AND WISHES. But decided to let it slide, b/c she seemed really nice.

Which reminds me of this fucking effing ENERGY JUICE (enerjuice) that I had on the way to this blackmetal show (in the woods, in America) which was made of 100% JUICE* (*containing "fruit or vegetable juice, sucralose, or other ingredients")

…(puzzled silence)

"OTHER INGREDIENTS?" You can't just DO THAT. That's like putting "etc." on an ingredient list. That informs me of basically nothing. OTHER INGREDIENTS?

That is like saying, "the only things in this juice are things that are in this juice." It's like logically defining a set as "all things which are contained in this set." Don't worry, man, at least you know that nothing that is not in that juice is in that juice.

Jesus.

Also, it's fucking freezing in the Maritimes. What is it, like eighteen degrees right now? Good thing I only brought shorts because last weekend I gored my knee open and now I am Incapable of Wearing Pants. At least I did remember to bring socks.

Also, delicious gluten-free fruit pie.

—

11:17pm: still more ALLNIGHTER CHEESEBURGERS and more VITAMIN WATER, prolonged discussion of the essentialist tendencies in German v. Scandinavian music:

a. What's with the Germans? Why do they try to recover their mystical transhistorical essence every, like, 10 yrs (Wagner, the Romantics, Heidegger, Nazism, krautrock)?

b. Specifically krautrock v. black metal. Why are the Scandanavians so much less romantic? Why they so sad?

—

(It's possible a day or so passes in here. Let's say no less than 1, no more than 1 1/2)

Discovering that Keith's White is mildly abominable, reminiscent of a soapy glass used to hold the perpetual dregs of a Screwdriver, the ice of which has melted. Watery, indistinct. Unsurprisingly I have to pee again.

Seriously, Keith's White is probably the worst "beer" I have ever tasted. I don't know how it even took me this long to realize that Keith's is totally shitty. Recently someone defended it to me in terms of "Had it not been for Keith's

I never, in the wasteland of Canadian and Labatt Blue in which I lived, would have been able to persevere in my deep spiritual belief that beer was something likeable, so in that respect I have a place for it in my heart," which is cool — that, I can get behind. But Jesus, it really is bad, and I drink like, Old Milwaukee Dry and PBR and Budweiser on occasion. Perhaps still worse is that it passes itself off as an IPA, which it most certainly is not, or I suppose is just legitimately the worst IPA ever. For babies. Babies who like to barf.

I even thought for a moment this summer that I liked it, because it reminded me of being a kid. Not actually drinking it, I just had a natural inclination in my youth toward products with animal logos—see also, when cornered by some/any male peer asking what hockey team I liked, I would invariably say the Penguins, maybe the (Buffalo) Sabers, and in later years, I suppose the San Jose Sharks or Anaheim Mighty Ducks, the latter of which I even had a t-shirt of. As if I knew one damned thing about hockey, NHL '94 being pretty much the extent of detail I was capable of, visually if not conceptually. Anyway, it turned out (re: liking Keith's) that a. I was wrong and b. Moosehead is totally better, and also has an animal on the bottle. A moose.

—

"I just feel like I paid $7 for the experience of eating a Louisiana-style cream sauce seafood crepe from a Der Schnitzelmann wagon in a parking lot in Sackville, New Brunswick at 12:35am. Like, now that I can say that, the materiality of the thing is totally beside the point."

—

1:27am: in half-hearted search for real schnitzel we end up at the AULAC BIG STOP, trapped behind a Berry-Go-Round laden transport truck. If you can believe it.

(Well, this thing basically writes itself, eh?)

———

Aug 3rd: Salmon with mayo and cheese, white wine, Growers, slaw, salsa, broccoflower. Bobby Hebb died today.

I was all geared up to write about mayonnaise, poor people food, and "gastronomic drift[2]", but it turns out the actual historical evidence for my intended argument was, you know, nonexistent. Which is a shame, because it would have gone like this: see, as we were driving back from the beach, my friend Sam and I decide, "Hey, the last time we saw each other we were both vegan—we should buy some goddamn salmon for dinner tonight!" and of course, PEI being for once in its frigging life obliging, within twenty-seven seconds of thinking this we drive by this shack with a big ol' FRESH FISH sign, and pop in, pick up some nice pink salmon filets, and we're on our way, happy as clams. We get back to her shack (okay, it's a house, really, a wonderful little house, but it's in the middle of the woods and has no electricity or running water. So, shack?) and her boyfriend is like "oh, I'll take care of this, an old family recipe," sautés up some onions and garlic, proceeds to slather the salmon in mayonnaise, tosses it all together with a couple of slices of cheese, and hucks it in the oven for about a half hour.

---

2 Not a real term, but I find it a useful one for thinking about how foods and their preparations move within and across cultures, less in terms of the concrete mechanisms of their dissemination (trade, colonialism, Papal decree, etc.) than the associations that they accrue. Effectively, how the meanings of *foods as texts* shift, in not always consistent or predictable fashion.

Now I know what you're thinking, because people keep saying it to me, but shut up for a moment, because that shit was delicious. I know, blah blah blah, covering a good piece of fish with mayo and baking the hell out of it is some kind of sacrilege, but it was hands down in the top five salmon-based meals I've had in my life.

The boyfriend was all half-apologetic, like, "yeah, it's pretty ghetto, but I like it," and I of course am like, "no dude, it rules," because in my head I'm thinking (on top of how it ruled) about the disproportionate amount of shit-talking mayo is subjected to despite its fairly honourable seat just off to the side of the French Mother Sauces of Escoffier's classification (it's really like one protein away from hollandaise, which gets way more cred). On the basis of which, I begin to develop the idea that more than likely this mayonnaise'd salmon recipe is some derivation, trickled down the line, of an older, more austere French dish. I mean, when you think about it, heavy sauce and all, it seems very believably French.

But as it turns out, as far as I can tell this is not the case. I spent a good little while poking around old French cookbooks, doing web research, etc., and didn't come up with anything even cut from a similar cloth. I'd like to think I just missed it, but I can admit when I'm wrong.

It was, however, delicious. Fuck the academy, fix me up with some mayo 'n fish 'n cheese. Seriously. There is certainly a place for salmon tartare, but I know who I'm gonna put my money on when shit gets heavy.

—

Aug 7th, 1:05am: twice in one night — once on a boat, again at The Old(e) Triangle, I ordered Té Bheag by its name, properly pronounced (chey vek), to be met by the blankest musterable looks. I mean, I guess I can't blame the Old Triangle, they are Irish, and thus should have no truck with Gaelic, right? RIGHT?

Does this make me a snob? I am increasingly inclined to the realization that "yes I am" over the course of this trip, but this is not one of those times.

Intensely Irish bar. Intensely unpronounceable name. How do you NOT make the effort?

By way of a little translation, my rationale here was that yes, it is a pretty unpronounceable name, and bartenders got a lot of other shit to deal with, they don't need some asshole blah blah blah (not like I would ever call a bartender on something like that—what do I look like, The Worst Dude?), but really, that almost makes it worse. Because a) you're a *bartender*, where's your pride? Your job is booze. Where's your sense of the craft? b) the fact that it is a curious name with no *immediately intuitive* key to its pronunciation, means that the chances of someone reading it, thinking they know how it's pronounced, and just getting it wrong, are pretty slim. More than likely you look at it and go "huh" and then, presumably ask someone, or look on the internet, or, as I just noticed not fifteen minutes ago, look on the back of the bottle, where it's written.

Come on dude, I mean, *I'm on a boat.*

That Man Ate All Our Shrimp!
And Two Plastic Lobsters!

In September 2010, to mark the fiftieth anniversary of the coining of the term cyborg, Tim Maly of Quiet Babylon[1] curated the 50 Posts About Cyborgs Project. I contributed an essay about *The Terminator* and cyborg ontologies, that had nothing at all to do with food, but in the process of trying to sort out what I was going to write about, I got to thinking about the age-old fantasy of the future which I like to refer to in shorthand as the *space-food-pill*. This is the idea I think we've all heard at one time or another of, "Wouldn't It Be Great If They Could Invent One Pill That Would Give You All Your Nutritional Requirements So You'd Never Have To Waste Time Cooking Or Eating Again?" (I'm sure you can guess how I feel about that sort of thing). To varying degrees, this idea has preoccupied us for some time, reoccurring regularly in sci-fi, but also taking shape in the "real world" as dehydrated "astronaut food," and to a certain extent, the supplements boom. By which I mean not merely vitamins, but superfoods like blue green algae and the like, supplements that *dream of being substitutes*; and the comparable reductionism of the juice diet.

What does this have to do with cyborgs? Well, maybe lots, maybe nothing, depending on how you think about cyborgs/what you use cyborgs to think about. It's a bit of a bigger discussion, and beside my central point, so I'll try

---

1 *Quiet Babylon: Cyborgs, Architects, and Our Weird Broken Future.* http://quietbabylon.com/

to condense it as effectively as possible, because it's still worth thinking about.

There's a lot of (academic) literature that goes beyond thinking cyborgs as just dudes with robot arms or, less fantastically, people with cochlear implants. Donna Haraway famously reinvigorated the term by using it simultaneously as a means to theorize hybridity, decentre the Enlightenment Subject, and conceptually explore humans' relationships to technology. Her work, and the theory-mill that it spawned both goes beyond and returns to the ambiguity of the term's original formulation, which included, along with synthetic/mechanical enhancements and other less predictable methods, the use of drug regimes to cybernetically alter the body's physiology. Cyborg technologies in this formulation were means of intervening and adapting the body to its environment (in this case, space).

If you think about it, this isn't such a stretch. Most drugs are synthetically derived little chemical engines which we take into the body that then disseminate into, and change the functioning of our bodies, in some cases on a permanent basis. An immediate criticism of this drugs-as-cyborg-technology position is, "Well, if drug use is cyborg, how is food use not? Food does basically the same thing, and in a more intimate way is actually responsible for building, re-building, and maintaining the human body." Pretty much the only non-totally-arbitrary response is that drugs at least satisfy the condition of being a form of synthetic technology, thus evoking (if only subtly) the old man/machine or organic/synthetic dialectic.

Unfortunately it is increasingly easy, and in fact increasingly inevitable, to make the counter-argument that as much food is genetically modified, the synthetic/organic and natural/technological binaries don't make such substantive distinctions (you can follow this further by asking, if genetically modified plants qualify as cyborgs, do we then become cyborgs by eating cyborgs?).

So, at the risk of saying We're All Already Cyborgs (which despite this exposition, I am loath to do, for reasons I'll get into some other time), the speculated hyper-synthetic, or hyper-technologically-mediated sustenance of the space-food-pill seems, if not an ideal candidate for wearing a little ceremonial cyborg hat, at the very least relevant to considerations of cyborg implications for food.

Okay, so that was less effectively condensed than I had intended.

And, as I said, sort of beside the point. Because *my* futuristic food fantasy is of a different stripe altogether. In fact, the very opposite—I long for a cyborg adaptation, be it nanotech or remote-controlled microenzymes or a little gastro-fusion reactor, or just a pimped out colostomy bag, that would allow one to eat vastly more than what the stomach would normally accommodate, and either convert this rapidly into energy stores, or fuck it, just burn it off via some outtake valve or like a flamethrower attachment. But the point is that you don't get full. Not that you don't get fat, really, I don't much care about that, although I suppose if such technology did exist it could more beneficially be put toward weight regulation for those with serious problems rather than just further indulging my conscienceless crapulent excesses.

But just think of it—think of how much you could eat without ever pushing yourself to that perilous state of nigh-comatose discomfort and self-loathing. It would be glorious! Perhaps there could be a regulator as well so one could enjoy copious amounts of alcohol without, you know, getting so drunk you pass out or die.

You could even have a component that allowed you to control how hungry you were, and thus the types and textures of desire, need, and appreciation you brought to the meals you consumed. There is an argument in here about a coming of age for the "art of eating" (or more appropriately a *techne* of eating) as distinct from the art of cooking, but I'm not going to make it. I'm not here to spoon-feed you, right?

Of course I am aware that in this era of already pathological overconsumption and food distribution inequalities such a suggestion is borderline offensive to humanity, but fuck it, so's the idea that someone would rather take a pill every day than *taste anything ever again*.

And it's not like I could afford it. It'd just be one more component of the magical fantasy world that the magically fantastically rich already live in, helping to align the spirit of the Roman vomitorium[2] with that of owning twenty-five cars. I mean, they already *eat gold* and get snake venom injected in their face, what are we even talking about?

---

2 Which apparently didn't actually exist (at least not the way I mean 'em here). So let's say… "helping to finally realize our fantasy of Roman decadence as represented by the popular misunderstanding of the 'vomitorium'…"

Words of Deep Concern
I Imagine I Once Sent

For whatever structural reasons, I seem to end up, as I am currently, drunk and alone in my brother's house more often than my own (correction—*getting* and *staying* drunk and alone), and as such, a notable amount of my writing has emerged flanked by his gigantic cats, toy robots, tastefully arranged clutter, and the just right number of decorative bottles that I have somehow never managed to capture in my own life. The first week, more or less, of my blog's existence, my late-night discovery of Julia Child's twenty second omelette recipe, probably a bunch of stuff about fennel and/or rapini, because cheap fennel and rapini season often coincides with my brother needing a cat-sitter; I cannot discount this house in the framing of my creative production.

I've also made some good meals here, in spite, even in outright defiance, of the sparseness of their stores; I bought my second cutting board to spare myself the spirit-rattling clatter of cutting vegetables upon the naked tile counters (I used torn-up beer boxes for a while, but enough is enough, you know?); and years ago, when homeless and affectedly derelict, I paid my board with grilled cheese sandwiches on demand, *grace à* the health food dumpster down the street, so generous with their waste that we had to stack the loaves several deep in the balcony's snow.

But it would be unfair to trace the gastronomic character of this place so solipsistically. It is true that I have heaped upon him what dangerously approaches a scornful incredulity for his ability to happily survive off of little more than instant coffee (in prodigious quantities) and bags of chips, but the fact remains that my brother has had a profound impact upon my eating habits: we are both "bad with chips," he brought me for the first time to a Montréal *bagelrie* (although I don't remember whether it was *Fairmount* or *St-Viateur*, only trudging through the snow, and then eating hot bagels and cold tzatziki in a bare room with a confused cat in Outremont), together we have consumed countless boxes of Breaktime Ginger Snaps until we both were intimately acquainted with the raw and lacerated mouths that attends such indulgence, and the Jade Garden all-you-can-eat-buffet will forever be associated with the bad decisions that he and I have made together (such as going to the Jade Garden all-you-can-eat-buffet. I don't think I am out of line in setting "no pizza" as one of my ground rules for attending a Chinese food buffet).

Above and beyond all these, my brother has exerted two still greater influences upon my gastronomic development. The first being that he *introduced me to dumpster diving*. Back in, hell, probably 1997, not out of any devotion he had to the political or lifestyle rhetoric that I later infused it with, but because he was a Fine Arts undergrad and had found a way to obtain *garbage bags full of donuts for free*—the acquisition of large quantities of donuts being the basic principle from which much of the Campbell Sons' practicality was to be derived. And I must say that this first dumpstering experience changed the terms. At the risk of hyperbole, but in deference to the fact that it's 3:47am and I've got about a litre of bad wine in me, it was like robbing a bank, in the way that suddenly the usual order of things had changed, one suddenly had access to things one never did before, by very different means than those one had come to think necessary and inevitable. And I don't know if you've ever had a garbage bag full of donuts on your living room floor, but *that is a lot of donuts*.

Trust me, that shit'll change you. To say nothing of the fact that thereafter one lives in a world where one can eat out of the garbage, and the whole Principle of Scarcity begins to seem profoundly chimerical.

The second influence, which dates to around the same time, even perhaps the same visit, was my brother making dinner for us by boiling some spaghetti, then *frying it up on a hot plate with Patak's curry paste*, before adding the tomato sauce. I don't remember if he added anything to the tomato sauce or whether it was just whatever can or jar was readily available, nor can I say with any certainty whether it was really more delicious than any other spaghetti I had eaten before; but I was in *My Big Brother's Apartment* in *The City* eating what I understood to be his *signature dinner*, so of course it tasted better than any spaghetti before-what are you, new? Fraternal piety aside, it was important because it taught me that you can *do things* to food—things that any number of people (in this example: myself, now) would tell you not to do, or even be too mortified to comment upon, but sometimes you just have to dump some herbs and some paste on that and fry it up—like, "fuck it, Imma Put A Egg In It[1]," you know? I am *convinced* that one of the

---

1 "I realized today that I've taken to putting eggs into other foods primarily as a signifier of my good mood—a 'fuck it, Imma Put A Egg In It' sort of thing. Like a little dude—gastronomy and whimsy and outright deliciousness all at once." (Mike Leo Lecky, 02.11.10)

"Also, to further my egg thing, IF YOU LIKE IT THEN YOU SHOULDA PUT A EGG IN IT. As sung by Beyonce." (03.11.10)

better angels of our nature, which along with restraint, and taste, and discretion, cannot be neglected but to our detriment, is just givin' er.

Anyway, all this to say: Zac, I ate all your butter. I mean, not "all" of it, but like, a *lot* of it. I always do. I wonder why you never write me after I've cat-sat and say, "Hey, by the way, where did all our butter go? Did you really eat a *pound* of butter in three days, or did you forget and let the cats go lickin' on it? You know we have pies to bake up in here, occasionally?"

You know, I didn't even used to *like* butter.

Not Much Pluck[1]

My dear mother recently called me out for beginning to manifest the "silly, stupid (masculine) bravado of engaging in who can eat the weirdest thing." To be fair to her, and myself, it was just shy of a calling-out; more a note of caution lest I slip into a tired and trite relationship with the bounty of the earth's board. I, unsurprisingly, am inclined to give myself more credit than that, although I am not insensitive to the risks. It is not that I have "nothing to prove"—we all have something to prove—but toughness and traditional masculinity, after a lifetime of being realistically beyond my (weak, effete) grasp, are not high on the list. Nor do I see myself as one who seeks the thrills of danger; I am a rather fearful type: of heights, teenagers, the Amazon; or even one

---

1 A confession: nearish to press time and still lacking a title for this piece, I turned to MFK Fisher's "The Trouble With Tripe" (from *With Bold Knife and Fork*, 1968) in hopes of finding some inspiration. Therein I came across a number of terms for offal with which I was not previously acquainted. Most notably, "lights" as what I suppose is a euphemism for lungs, and "pluck," referring, according to the OED, to "The heart, liver, and lungs (sometimes with other viscera) of a beast, as used for food." It is upon the leeway of, "sometimes with other viscera" (and its pleasingly apposite homonymy) that I stake the legitimacy of my employing it here, although I am happy to have my etymological suspicions confirmed by the following reference, from the *Edinburgh Evenings News* of the 28th of June, 1904: "The Sheriff inquired the meaning of the word 'pluck'. The prosecutor explained that it referred to the internal organs which could be removed at one pull or pluck, the liver, lungs and heart." Whether or not this explanation is apocryphal, it is therefore no great mystery that "plucky" has come to mean much the same thing as "gutsy," even if the roots of the expression have grown shrouded to all but the butcher set. A close runner-up for the title was "Something Offal."

who particularly likes a challenge.[2]

But amidst such protestations I cannot deny that I historically have had some inclinations toward extremism. I was at one time both straightedge and vegan, and post breaking-edge and breaking-veg I have run the gamut from common lush to budding oenophile and scotch aficionado, and become quite an avid and energetic omnivore. And it is in fact in what I believe to be the honest and best spirit of omnivory that I pursue what sometimes amounts to gastronomic excess. Just as my time as a spice-lover (after a body-terrifying experience with a level-five Vietnamese chicken curry soup and a bottle of cheap *Gewürztraminer*, I have downgraded myself to a modest "spice-friend") was motivated by a sincere love for the taste and tastes of spice (for I persist, against the haters, supertasters, and apologists for mildness, that most any case of "all you can taste is spicy" is in the head of the taster, not a limitation that has been imposed by/upon the dish itself), so too have my forays into organ meats, offal, and other odds and ends been inspired foremost by a love for and curiosity about flavour. How am I to know what a goose foot tastes like until I have tried it? Perhaps I'll love it! (It turns out I do not.) But beyond mere pleasure-seeking, I am motivated as well by what I suppose is pride. For where the sketchier bits of animals are concerned, I cannot but feel that it is intellectual dishonesty to turn up one's nose so readily. Perhaps that is unfair. I do not mean to begrudge anyone their squeamishness. I mean to say that such dietary prescriptions that allow us to categorize offal as revolting and unfit

---

2 I recently realized that I do not like to be challenged, I prefer to take something manageable and quite within my capacities and needlessly make it more difficult for myself. It is much more satisfying to move a mountain than a molehill, and no less so when one the mountain is of one's own making.

for consumption are by and large culture-and class-bound, and while I am not so naive as to believe that we can with one fell swoop dash such subject-positioning structures to bits, I personally feel behoved to try. Particularly when the results may be delicious.

Do not mistake me for one who claims a snobbish victory over those poor hegemonic diners who quail at exotic fare only to revel in my own self-satisfied and abominable fetishism, though, please. As far as the cultivation of the self goes, I am merely *interested* in tasting what lies beyond the curtain of my own commonplace; I do not judge others for their tastes so long as they do not pretend to speak to and through some moral dinnerary absolute. A rather considerate friend of mine makes a point of not referring to foods as "gross," instead specifying that she does not like them as a matter of preference rather than ontology. She does this out of a concern for the intimacy and importance of food, and the profound judgement implied by disgust—profound because it is precisely an evaluation that sets itself up as pre-political but is more often than not quite the contrary. Indeed, disgust may be the most insidiously hegemonic of performances. By which I do not mean that it is put-on or insincere, but that by smuggling them in through the very gut that we are supposed to trust, disgust can safeguard certain prejudices from critical examination. Taste may be intensely personal, but that does not preserve it from being ideological. The way to a man's heart is through his stomach, after all.

But how does it actually work, disgust? I am not satisfied with the explanation that it is simply a technology of ethnocentrism, classism, or racism, for those are but attributions, not explanations, and are frankly less interesting than exploring what else goes on behind the crinkled nose, what other discourses are enrolled in its justification.

I recently ate at a Russian restaurant a halved hard-boiled egg, topped with roe. In a later discussion a friend found the very idea of the thing disgusting, and said that the first association that came to mind was that it seemed somehow *cannibalistic*. Now on the surface this is absurd, or at least inaccurate. It is no more or less cannibalistic than eating either a hard boiled egg or roe on their own, and neither should logically be any more disgusting than the other, being exactly the same thing, just of different animals. Indeed, it "should" be no different from any other meat and meat combination (the club sandwich, bacon cheeseburger, English breakfast, etc.), merely at a different stage in the life cycle. Chicken and fish, but unfinished, just the raw material, as it were. She countered that it so happened that she was not a big fan of meat on meat in the first place, and the conversation drifted elsewhere, fairly enough.

To take it further, I can see how on another level this does make associative sense. The egg 'n' roe discomfort seems to derive from a sense of dangerous and unsettling proximity, a combination that is somehow "too close for comfort." Which is arguably part of the disturbing *frisson* of cannibalism. Of course cannibalism, as with all taboos that rely upon insider-outsider distinction, depends on boundaries that are protean, contingent, and historically and culturally variable. As with incest, the other famous "universal" taboo, anthropologists have long identified that while the prohibition is ubiquitous, species-membership and kinship are variously determined, such that who counts as human and therefore inedible, or family and therefore unfuckable, is by no means self-evident according to our definitions. Nonetheless, in a sense, the logic proceeds along the lines of, cannibalism = you should not eat someone/something that is so close to you that it is almost you; incest = you should not couple with someone that is so close to you that they are almost you. Thus there is *something* in the proximity (both physical and typical) of the roe n' egg that in its discomfort echoes this; it cannot be mapped on precisely, but the traces are legible, if distorted (by what? A sense of the vulnerability of the egg? The unforeseeable dangers of meddling with the not-yet-fully-formed, as with genetic engineering and child sexuality?). Perhaps it is precisely the inconsistency that cannot be explained, but associative links are not in themselves worthless for their categorical ambiguity.

The spectre of cannibalism was invoked again over a lunch I passed recently with a colleague, in this case regarding a plate of calf brains sautéed in *buerre brun* with capers and sage.[3] Curious to try the dish, and in fact utterly enchanted by the flavour, her response was nonetheless, "I feel totally cannibalistic eating this." But why, why?! Zombies? Is it because of zombies? Because that is a train of associations I suppose I can follow. Zombies are certainly the most visible denizens of the public imagination to regularly feast on brains,[4] and to the extent that we do not deny the living dead their human status, they consequently qualify as cannibals. And of course, prior to the modern concept of the zombie, zombies were strongly associated with voodoo, which emanating from the ineffable Blackness of European fantasy has the cannibalistic savage waiting slavering in the wings, if not already present.

---

3 So delicate a name as *cervelles* (the feminization/diminutive of the French word for brains) is a prime example of the old bit of down-to-earthism that "You give it a pretty, French name and suckers will eat anything."

So fallacy or no, it could go something like this: Zombies eat brains. Zombies are cannibals. Ergo, eating brains is cannibalistic. As skeptical as I am of this link, I will admit that even I sometimes confusedly think of movies like *Cannibal Ferox* as zombie films, if only for the company they keep.

As an interesting twist upon the cultural specificity of cannibalism(s), it has been argued that zombies cannot rightly be considered cannibals, because something in the process of becoming the undead severs of the bonds of species. Zombification then amounts to a sort of *speciation*, a redrawing of the lines of self and other and a rearticulation of the terms of recognition that accounts for zombies not simply devouring each other. The living dead are thus no longer in continuity with the living (we are familiar with these ideas in the case of vampires), but in competition, with unique physiology, dietary needs, and reproductive

4 It is perhaps testament to the disruptive power of cerebrophagy (not a real word) that the zombie-as-brain-eater has so firmly taken root in popular culture, given that this permutation of the zombie is of so particular and recent pedigree. Whereas we can place the birth of the "modern" zombie, as inarticulate, shambling corpse that feeds on the flesh of the living with George Romero's 1968 *Night of the Living Dead*, it is not until Dan O'Bannon's 1985 *Return of the Living Dead* that the idea of the zombie hungry specifically for brains is introduced. As much as I resent *Return* for planting the seeds of the "fast zombie" that has grown to be so obnoxiously ubiquitous with films like *28 Days Later* and Zack Snyder's *Dawn of the Dead* remake, O'Bannon manages to bring a genuine pathos to the zombie in a scene where the beleaguered humans are able to interrogate a zombie chained to a table. For all that *Return* plays zombies for laughs (tag line, "They're back from the grave and ready to party!"), it is quite chilling when the zombie haltingly explains that it eats brains ("Not people, brains") in order to relieve the "pain of being dead." Suddenly we see zombies not as mere monsters, but again as human beings, *feeling* human beings who are trapped in dead, decaying bodies, feeling the blood pool in their extremities, the worms that chew their flesh, and are driven mad by the agony. Through which the one thought that resounds, loud and clear, is *brains*. Brains will ease the pain.

incompatibility to seal the deal. But I suppose this is a little beside the point.

It can't be all zombies, I guess, this brain-eating qualmishness, but where else to look for insight? In the brain itself? Is there something in (or rather, of) the brain, as an emblem of our differentiation from the "lower" animals (more so, arguably, than our dextrous hands) that strikes one as too close to home? Is the brain the face that, being our own, is the hardest to face? Or is it just that in our techno-secular metaphysical hand-wringing, the brain is the likeliest candidate for a seat of the soul, and thus such similarity suggests just a little more commonality with the lower orders than we are comfortable with?

Shit, I dunno. But in the midst of all of this it occurs to me that there has been a fundamental shift in my relationship to food over the past few years. Namely that *disgust* now plays a profoundly diminished role in determining what I eat. Rather, I no longer make a place for disgust in my thinking about food, and when and where it attempts to assert itself, I subject it to a sound rationalist beating about the face and neck before I will submit to its influence. As potentially unhealthy as it may sound, I suppose I am proud that I think twice before I trust my own disgust.[5]

But thinking twice only gets one so far. For in my organ-eating adventures I have come up against a phenomenon both formidable and puzzling—pure *post facto* (or perhaps *per facto*, "during the fact") physical disgust. Which is to say that I am gradually coming to be of the opinion that I "have a hard time with organ meats." This despite my willingness at the level of principle (the principles of equality—no part of an animal shall be judged as less worthy of consumption than another by any standard than that of taste) to embrace them.

Having a fairly staid meat-eating existence prior to becoming vegetarian, I entered the fray with quite an admirable potential for new experiences. My experience with organ meats or other kinds of offal was restricted to the haziest of recollections of not being super keen on liver, but that was about it.

A few months ago I was at a restaurant well-renowned for its in-house, nose-to-tail butchery, and I ordered the devilled kidneys on toast.

"Do you like kidneys?" my lunch date inquired, and to my reply that I didn't know, for I wasn't sure I'd ever tasted them, responded, "Well, be careful—they're good, but really intense. A friend of mine had them here and it fairly blew out his palate for the rest of the day."

This, coupled with my faintly shimmering hangover, should have given me pause, or rather, the pause this gave me should have translated into an order of something a little

5 This has not always been the case. Although even when I was vegan I was of the cloth that "eating animals does not strike me as wrong as such—it is the cruelty and injustice fostered in the process that I resist," I was still quick to declaim in rather moralizing terms foods that I thought were downright disgusting (Clamato juice and sour cream were two favourite targets), for at heart I am something of a judgemental fucker (I prefer to see it as a "principled criticism") and even then showed a similar flare for oratorical hyperbole. But what relationship does this bear to my late carnivory? Is it an inevitable consequence of the type of slackening opprobrium necessary to make the shift from vegan to omnivore? Or was it part of some broader change in orientation that allowed this transition in the first place? In order to return to meat-eating at all a new personal threshold of revulsion was necessary (or causal), and it could be that disgust fell to the wayside before the success of a program the rigour of which demanded that if I was going to eat animals, it would not do to be finicky and particular about, as it were, "the nasty bits." Certainly my own turn toward the aestheticization of excess in my early twenties (roughly simultaneous with my starting to drink) played a facilitating role, although it's hard to say whether that was an influence or a outcome of my quite predictable trajectory from extreme asceticism to extreme indulgence. I suppose I blame Jean Genet.

more mild-mannered, but no, I went ahead and ordered the kidneys, and no sooner than the first bite was ninety-five percent convinced that I would be unable to take another, let alone finish the dish. Luckily, she being of sterner stuff than myself, my friend obligingly traded her own breakfast of house-cured bacon, eggs, *fevès au lard*, and *boudins* both *blanc* and *noir*, that happily I was able to dispatch with aplomb.

Two things were striking about this experience. The first was that despite my professed skepticism about taste and total recall,[6] with that first bite came a flash of recognition that immediately transported me back several years and across an appreciable expanse of ocean. I was with a friend in Palermo and we had found our way to what was reputedly one of the oldest *focaccerias* in Italy. I don't recall what we actually ate as our meal (except that we finished it with some very respectable cannoli), but we were fixated by the spectacle of a man in the centre of the vaulted stone dining room working over an immense steaming pot of... something. He was armed with a large stirring utensil that apparently sported just enough of an edge that he could alternate scooping chunks of what appeared to be lard from the gigantic block thereof on his left, and some mysterious mass of pressed-together meat[7] on his right, both of which

---

6 See "In Which Two Edith Wharton Characters Admit To Mutual and Increasingly Shattering Betrayals"

7 For years I assumed it was some kind of liver, because it seemed to ring some rusty bell in the far off reaches of my brain that associated that taste with what I remembered of liver. One day while reading a magazine article on Sicilian cuisine, I came across a passing reference to what sounded like the *focacceria* we had been to, so renowned for its sandwiches. It took some investigative work that I am moderately proud of, including a lot of puzzling over translation of Italian words for animal parts, but I eventually solved the mystery of said sandwich. Pecorino, lard, lung and spleen of veal.

he would throw into the pot. Meat. Lard. Stir. Repeat. His other duty was to provide made-to-order sandwiches that consisted of a roll torn open and spread with more lard, a helping of meat, and a fistful of some coarsely-grated hard cheese that I assumed to be pecorino or parmigiano.

I was not a committed meat eater at the time, but nor was I any longer a committed vegetarian, and so I could not resist the beauty and simplicity of such a sandwich as this. I purchased one, went in for a taste (I waited until we were outside, thankfully), and I swear before my teeth even had a chance to meet and complete the bite, spit it out into the street.

"It's not bad... I just can't eat it," I explained, explaining nothing. Luckily, this time also I was accompanied by a friend who, were I so shameable, would have put me to shame by her ability to enjoy such fare.

"This," she spoke through gravy-stained lips, "is possibly the most delicious thing I have ever eaten."

This brings us back to the second thing that was strange about the devilled kidneys on toast, which I was not able to fully articulate at the time. I remember saying, while passing the dish of kidneys across the table, that I could fully understand why this food was good and how people found it delicious, but I was nonetheless unable to eat it. It was not until many months later, when at the same restaurant (lessons learned? Fie!) I ordered the calf brains with capers and sage that I fully realized that there was something to the taste of much organ meat that I really couldn't handle, even if I otherwise found the food quite pleasing. For here again I was only able to have a couple of bites in total, and again was saved by my companion who in spite of her own psychological difficulties with the idea of eating brains ("It feels cannibalistic"), found the taste itself irresistible.

Whereas I, who had no conceptual difficulties, and in fact believed strongly in the idea of eating offal, found the brains delicious, but inedible. This has been a bit of a hard thing for me to get my head around, but it seems to best express the situation. Most acutely in the case of the brains, I found the taste overall to be quite pleasing, but there was something, some strange quality of richness,[8] that I have a difficult time even identifying in accordance with my existing lexicon of tastes, and that my body seems to reject wholly of its own accord.[9]

I have chosen to accept this paradox because it opens up an interesting space where desire, pleasure, taste, and appreciation no longer rest in as easy and predictable relationship to each other as was previously presumed. Am I "turned off" of organ meats, however? Can the answer be both yes and no? I will not likely order brains again anytime soon, but that is by no means certain. Even at the time, I had my own suspicions that perhaps had I not been remotely hung over, or had I been already steeped in some luxurious sensuality, I would have been more ready to appreciate the richness. Perhaps if I ate them at night? Or you know, maybe not. The case of tripe presents another puzzle. I have often heard it described as a very difficult piece of meat to enjoy, with nonetheless its cult of devotees, but I have enjoyed it many times within the context of a bowl of pho, which for all its aromatic complexity is still funda-

---

8 There is also, more in the case of the kidneys, the lung and spleen, and some blood sausage, than with the brains, a sort of "tastes like dust" association that I have. I know that dust and richness are not usually considered kith, let alone kin, but I can't seem to shake it.

9 I know that I'm excluding here all consideration of sub- or un-conscious inhibitions, but shit, I can't think of any more boring a way of resolving this than, "Maybe I'm subconsciously not okay with eating organs."

mentally a dish topped with pretty unadorned meats; and I think that this lured me into a false confidence when it came to my ability to appreciate other types of offal. Still I cling doggedly to the idea that this is not so much a matter of trying to prove something as it is a curiosity about the particularities and the contingencies of one's own limits, and around these limits, the potentialities for gustatory enjoyment. As I said before that I like to think twice before I trust my intellectual disgust, I am not in any final way *convinced* by my physical disgust.

It is, I hope, not in the spirit of unflappable masculine fortitude then that I will continue eating somewhat off the beaten path, but out of a *willingness to believe* that there is a sort of truth in the tastes of others, and that in being able to share that taste (here I mean both taste as preference of the person, and taste as quality of the food), some small achievement can be made in the way of the chasm of irreducible difference that separates all people from one another becoming somewhat less yawning. So that when we greet each other across the abyss, you may not recognize my face, but the voice at least will be familiar.

In his essay "Fresh Figs"[1] Walter Benjamin states that "Gourmandizing means above all else to devour one thing to the last crumb. There is no doubt that it enters more deeply into what you eat than mere enjoyment." Rereading this of late, I found myself troubled by this use of "gourmandize." Is this what gourmandizing means after all? The voracity described seemed to jar against what I recalled of the Gastronomic Hierarchy, but further investigation proved not tso be especially enlightening:

> *The Gastronomic Hierarchy*
> (*from Schott's Food & Drink Miscellany*)
>
> *Gastronome* (*one with a serious interest in gastronomy*)
> *Gourmet* (*a connoisseur of food and drink*)
> *Friande* (*epicure*)
> *Gourmande* (*one who enjoys eating*)
> *Goulu* (*glutton*)
> *Goinfre* (*greedy-guts*)[2]

In fact, there is nothing inconsistent here with Benjamin's use; *goulu* may have served just as well. Indeed, he uses the term *gluttony* in the preceding sentence, and the tautologies and circularities that run rampant through the Hierarchy (see: *friande—epicurean* being defined by the

---

1 See "Food As Destroyer"

OED as "*devoted to the pursuit of pleasure; hence, luxurious, sensual, gluttonous. Now chiefly: devoted to refined and tasteful sensuous enjoyment.*" Italics mine. We're getting somewhere with refined and tasteful, but again slide back into the imprecision of gluttony.) impoverish it somewhat as a definitional authority. Nonetheless, the differentiation of the glutton and the gourmand seems worth maintaining, a point pursued with particular conviction by Jean Anthelme Brillat-Savarin, in his *The Physiology of Taste: Or, Meditations on Transcendental Gastronomy* (1825). In "On Gourmandism" he expresses his own dissatisfaction with prevailing dictionary definitions of *gourmandism*: "There is a perpetual confusion of *gourmandism* in its proper connotation with *gluttony* and *voracity*," and proceeds to offer his own: "Gourmandism is an impassioned, considered, and habitual preference for whatever pleases the taste. *It is the enemy of overindulgence*; any man who eats too much or grows drunk risks being expelled from its army of disciples." (Italics mine.) Here is the decisive break with Benjamin, or, to be fair, with the *translator* of Benjamin.

It is fitting that it is of the author of "The Task of the

---

2 I really like *goinfre*, and have been trying (unsuccessfully) to incorporate it into day-to-day speech. Especially since I discovered that it derives from the past participle of *se goinfrer*, which effectively means to feast excessively ("*manger beaucoup, gloutonnement, et malproprement*"). I haven't found any evidence of it functioning as an adjective, like *goinfré* to mean, "stuffed because of your own misproportioned and ill-considered gluttony" (uh, crapulence?), but since the verb is reflexive, I think I could get away with it, and just maybe come off as a wit in the process. I was hoping that *goulu* had a similar infinitive, something like *gouloir*, but no dice. Or at least it's not included in my *Petit Larousse*; although I did find it twice on dating websites: "*Amour. Estime. Gouloir.*" What? I choose to interpret that as meaning something like "Love. Respect. Fattening." But this is, as always, but idle speculation. (Dear The French, where are you when I need you? And why, when I do not, are you always singing karaoke SO LOUD across the street?)

Translator" that we start by asking "does this really mean what *he says* it means?" or "Is this *really* what he means?" before consulting what he in fact said prior to translation.[3] What is immediately striking is that Benjamin did *not* use the word gourmandize in the original text of "Fresh Figs". We could say that this is unsurprising, as Benjamin was writing in German and Brillat-Savarin claims that gourmandism "has no true name except the French one, *la gourmandise*; it cannot be designated by the Latin word *gula*, any more than by the English *gluttony* or the German *lusternheit*." However, Benjamin was fully fluent in French and had translated both Baudelaire and Proust, so we can safely bet that he was both familiar with *la gourmandise* and sensitive to the nuances the language. More to the point, not only did he not use *la gourmandise*, but neither did he employ some other specialized term (such as *lusternheit*, whatever that means. Lust for health? Life devourer?); he actually just wrote "*to eat.*"

"Fressen, das meint vor allem: Eines, mit Stumpf und Stiel."

Now in translating "eat" as "gourmandize," the translator tries to get at something that he feels may be lost in too direct, unadorned speech. Does he succeed or fail? What is funny to me is that in attempting to render Benjamin's *fressen* more faithfully into English, he resorts to a French word, that itself has a fraught and ambiguous meaning. Is this but a furbelow of translation, or is it considered and intentional? Is it an attempt to imbue the word with something of the mystery and history, the non-identity of the translated work, a bit of play with auratic perception? I

---

3 Fitting because of Benjamin's concern with the transformations of translation and the potential the practice holds for unleashing a "pure language" that goes beyond either style or brute information.

suppose I really don't care.

I must say though that there are places where the attempt to render a translation more true by resorting to idiom has almost the opposite effect for me. "To devour one thing to the last crumb" I pass over, almost with indifference; Benjamin's *stumpf und stiel,* "root and branch," by contrast immediately conjures something of the completeness with which the thing must be devoured. Perhaps it is just my romanticization of an unfamiliar language (for I assume that "to the last crumb" was chosen for its equivalent banality to the presumably equally idiomatic and bland "root and branch"), but "root and branch" lends both a totality and a temporality to the thing, as if, consistent with "I ate to destroy it," one seeks to wipe out not only the present but the *past* existence of the thing itself. It has a "Fuck it, let's do the whole village" sort of feel.

It Could Have Reminded
Me of a Lot of Things

Duck Eggs: I've been eatin' 'em. I was going to say that I am trying to expand my familiarity with the "raw material of life" food group, but I am actually trying to keep my semen and foetus consumption to a minimum. Eggs though? Oh boy. Growing up I never had that much of a fancy for eggs, with the possible exceptions of their roles in French toast and egg-in-a-hole (which I understand others know by the perfectly unnecessary euphemism "toad-in-a-hole"), and even my transition via eggs from veganism to vegetarianism a couple of years back was a little pitched. I began eating eggs again out of desperation, rather than affection, having been beset by persistent ill health that went unalleviated by other dietary experiments such as gluten freedom, Eating Right 4 My Blood Type, and not drinking all the time. So I was like, "Geez, alright! Maybe eggs? If I must?" and call it irrational fidelity to the party line, but despite becoming like seventy-five percent less sick all the time pretty much immediately after starting to eat eggs, I still resist attributing my improvement to that particular change in diet. Perhaps it is only in order to soften the extent to which I've sold out that I don't want to say something that can be taken as supporting the "You can't be truly healthy on a vegan diet" line that annoyed me for so many years.

It was some time into eating eggs again that I really began to embrace them. At first I could only eat fried eggs, and only so long as the yolk did not at any point rupture and spill onto the hot surface of the pan; otherwise I would be nauseated and unable to proceed. I am now very much over it, and enjoy eggs in as many forms as I can currently imagine, from poached to fried to *spaghetti alla carbonara* to Putting A Egg In It[1] (including my failed attempts to get an over-easy fried egg into a grilled cheese sandwich),which the French adorably refer to as *à cheval*. These last two are but slightly different manifestation of the same principle of betterment via a egg. *Carbonara*, as you probably know, involving (among other things) tossing a raw egg into freshly drained pasta, so the residual heat cooks it into a silky sauce, and *à cheval* describing the practice of topping something with a fried egg. The term literally translates into "on horseback," referring to how the egg atop the whatever, could be a steak, could be a __, looks like a little saddle! A little egg saddle!

Duck eggs, as it turns out, are considerably more expensive than hen eggs, but I thought what the hey, I love eggs and I hate ducks, so let's see what can be made of this. Duck eggs also have a slightly more oblong shape and sturdier shell then hen eggs, which has made for some hard times in the cracking, but I'm getting used to it. I had to stab one of them with a fork today, but don't take my ineptitude as representative. The yolks, at least as compared to the hen eggs that I regularly get, are a little paler and larger, and the whites somewhat more gelatinous. I described them to someone yesterday as "more like gristle" (eliciting predictable if unintended revulsion), but I think gelatinous says it better. They also remain a little more translucent, which unfortunately translates to looking a little grey, and seem less creamy. Duck eggs are apparently noted for their gami-

---

1 See "Words of Deep Concern I Once Sent"

ness, but I didn't notice any appreciable difference, and I'm sure it comes down to how and upon what feed they are raised. Overall interesting, but I don't feel compelled to go out of my way to continue eating them.

This whole Duck Egg Affair brings to my mind that *Far Side* comic where a bunch of animals are hanging out and one of them yells "Duck!" and they all duck as a duck flies overhead (as if thrown, not flying under its own power, which is essential to the comic's effectiveness). The comic, in turn, reminds me that I've been meaning to do some thinking about puns. Because I'm conflicted.

On the one hand, I disagree with Samuel Johnson's oft-quoted dismissal of the pun as the "lowest form of humour," because it simply isn't so[2]—puns rely on a facility with language of both the speaker and the listener, exploiting the ambiguities and polysemies of a given language in ways that may range from merely superficial homophonic resemblance to subtle historical, literary, or political significance. Puns need not be employed solely for humorous effect, for they occur all over the place from the Bible to Nabokov to military iconography, performing artful involutions that may be merely clever or form part of an architecture of symbolic depth and complexity. Punning, even at its worst

---

2 I'm not sure what I would consider the "lowest" form of humour-scat humour and slapstick offer themselves as likely candidates. Both of which I love, and which I think require a certain amount of artistry in order to be done right. Although even the qualifier "done right" suggests a certain amount of self-awareness or conversation with their own histories as forms of humour, which is totally a typically po-mo and academic (read: snobbish) thing to say. Like, "I like toilet humour, but only *smart toilet humour*." I'm not just saying "Oh, I love Rabelais and Charlie Chaplin, they were truly artists," because Gregory Peck tripping over a Barcalounger, or like, a guy falling off a building and landing on a toilet, preferably totally shattering the porcelain and his collarbone in the process, is pretty funny. Pretty, pretty, funny.

and certainly at its best, can be said to insinuate the spatial complexity and hidden structures of language (in general and in particular languages, in apparent isolation or in defiance of this appearance, in the case of interlingual puns).

On the other hand, I sometimes just want to throttle Shelagh Rogers and bomb the entire writing staff of CBC Radio's *As It Happens* off the face of the goddamn earth.

Because on *As It Happens* the punning is so frequent that it just feels mandatory and rote, as if they had a quota to fill. So what one ends up with is this deluge of seemingly awful (although perhaps not so bad if taken in the proper time, place, and proportion?) puns, and as with all humour, cooking, and I guess all of life, everything has its measure—sacrifice timing and discretion and you just have an obnoxious, tasteless (or noxious, abrasive) mess.

Newspapers are also terrible as well as, OFTLOG (Oh For The Love Of God), both themed mystery and paranormal romance novels (and paranormal romantic mysteries), although at least in the case of the latter two there isn't the same sense of the debasement of an otherwise serious and important medium. Not that I'm against debasement, necessarily, but, dudes, it can get pretty *heinous*. I don't know who established this as a trend, but terrible and indiscriminate pop culture and literary puns abound, spun to such an extreme that they no longer really refer to anything. Or when the choice of the title incorporating the reference often bears little or no relation to the content of the referent. "Demons Are A Ghoul's Best Friend"? Seriously?

I realize that I too trade both heavily and freely in puns, but for the sake of good taste, I try to rein it in. Every time I am tempted toward paronomasia, I stop and ask myself if there isn't an obscure or totally oblique literary or musical reference I could be using. Out of respect for the medium, and all that.

But why do I find Eggspectations more annoying than *Quoi De N'Oeuf*, as far as punned restaurant names go? Because of the French, the charming exoticism (or self-satisfaction of being able to understand) of a pun in a foreign language ("*quoi de neuf*" = "what's new?" although in my head the restaurant was always *Quoi D'Un Oeuf*, which would mean something like, "What, but an egg?" if it actually translated and was something people said, which I guess it isn't, but I still prefer it to reality)? They are both rather simple puns, involving no recursion or reference to anything other than a word or phrase and the fact that both places sell a lot of eggs. Even *L'Amère à Boire*, which I rather like, is not really that complex. "*Ce n'est pas la mer à boire*," a French expression, roughly "it's not like you have to drink the sea," means that something is not a big deal; *amère* is French for bitter, so it effectively conjures up the idea of a bar where you can hang out and chillax while drinking good beers, but is not itself rocket science. Perhaps I am just a snob.

Well-Corned

Well-Corned, *adjective* exhilarated with liquor

Which is to say, stoked in liquor. Or specifically, stoked with/by liquor. Although my OED does not draw this comparison, Ammon Shea notes the antonymy of the term "barleyhood," meaning drunk and mean. I'm not sure if that's a noun or an adjective, but I prefer it nominally, as in, "Don't even talk to Sherman right now, he's got his barleyhood up," or, "Back in the careless and bellicose days of my barleyhood, I smashed glass and burned bridges with joyless abandon, lo."

More specifically, it reminds me of years ago telephoning a friend, and his roommate answering "No, he's not here—I think he was on his way to your place, and he seemed rather drunk and bellicose."

"I Believe that's 'Reindeer'."
"No, That's Snow, Darling."

Our family did not have a wealth of distinct Christmas traditions, outside of participating in the standard array of secular-Christian, gift-giving, turkey-eating, family-tolerating activities. Two, however (the only two?), come to mind. The first, I do not know when it was established, but I'm going to throw 1986 out there, was that of my brother and I being allowed to open one present on Christmas Eve. This is not special in itself; I understand it to be a not uncommon way of checking the frantic agitation of greed that possesses many children at this time of year and reaches its almost unbearable apotheosis between 8:45pm and 3:00am Christmas Eve/morn.

Our especial gloss on the tradition was that our parents would always give us each amongst our presents an *advent calendar*, and that unfailingly my brother and I would choose that as our Christmas Eve present to open. Remembering this raises a host of questions—how did this get started? Why were we given advent calendars only on *the night before* Christmas, thus obliterating utterly their purpose and whatever distinguished them from any old box of chocolates? Were they *cheaper* closer to Christmas, as other calendars become by the month of March?

Of course, when one receives an advent calendar on the twenty-fourth, no other option exists than to eat all twenty-five of those barely-passing-as-chocolate chocolates in one fell swoop, or at most over the course of an hour or so. Such is the remaining quality distinguishing advent calendars from other boxes of chocolates when their intended temporal specificity is collapsed into an orgy of chocolate tablet consumption—*the form*. There is probably something exciting for a child in prying open the little cardboard hatches and popping the chocolates out of their little plastic bubble-molds, comparing to ensure that the illustration underneath accords with the given chocolate shape. I'm sure I remember failing to notice some or other compartment, to excitedly discover it later on or even the next day; an activity, a space of indeterminacy that could only open up when one is freed from the methodical procedure of opening and eating each chocolate on its own day. Honestly, I don't think that I even realized advent calendars had an intended use until nigh on adulthood, both "advent" and "calendar" long settled into the nominal opacity and meaninglessness that even the otherwise inquiring minds of children are wont to accept when chocolate is on the line.

I haven't had one in years, and it is perhaps just as well, for even through the fog of nostalgia I am conscious that advent calendar chocolate was pretty poor stuff, more than likely near the terminal point of the waxy or putty-like branch of the "chocolatey confection" family tree. That said, one might think that so practised a fool as myself could have taken it upon his self to assemble a couple of advent calendars for he and his brother, to lend a little of that nostalgia to this year's proceedings. But I am a mostly a *sentimental* fool, not primarily a *practical* one.

The second family tradition, which I have inexplicably failed to resuscitate since I have returned to the ranks of carnivory, was our Christmas morning breakfast: "hot mamas." This consisted of nothing more than bread with bacon and cheese on it, thrown under the broiler. If advent calendars enjoy an aura of nostalgic fondness, I am fairly blinded by that of the "hot mama." And perhaps therein lies my hesitancy to attempt a recovery—the keen awareness of the discrepancy between how special a thing seems at the time versus the likelihood of it being able to carry forward that quality into the cold light of the present.

Which for me makes the question of how something becomes "special" all the more intriguing. I don't think that we ever ate hot mamas other than Christmas morning, or if so it must have been very rarely. Perhaps bacon was uncommon in the house? Was this a dish that my brother and I had somehow gotten into, or was it a treat to our parents themselves? In any case, I certainly have not had hot mamas since, and face the prospect with some trepidation, if only because I am concerned that bacon and cheese on toast may not stand the test of time, may fail to invoke what I need it to invoke.

At which point it becomes clear that it is not about the snack and how good it is, but how much of that capacity for wonder, that ability to carry forward fond associations, persists in our own hearts. It becomes about not how good the food is, but how good *we* are, good at keeping something warm and familiar alive inside of ourselves, so that when we bring the food to our lips it is already pouring forth to enclose and infuse the item, fold it into an ongoing narrative of home, tradition, whathaveyou.

Much as I wish it otherwise, and if my attempts at sauerkraut, relationships, and the plants in my kitchen are any indication, keeping such things alive is not my strong point.

So I leave hot mamas aside, to rest unmolested in my memory. Christmas morning I pursue, in solitude, a breakfast satisfying to some senses, if unlikely to provide foundations for any new tradition. I have discovered red cress, which I had no idea existed and is perhaps the most beautiful "green" vegetable I have yet encountered. If you are unfamiliar, picture something not unlike regular watercress, but with the leaves consumed by a dusky, reddish, purple, shot through along the life-lines with bright green that could easily be misconstrued as representing, you know, "new hope" or something.

Red cress, chanterelles, walnuts. Merry Christmas.

Et Tu?

The Gin Caesar is a hell of a drink. I say this out of full respect for the tradition of the Bloody Caesar as a vodka drink. For all the stink I've made in casual conversation about the sanctity of the martini (if you turn "mar" into a disposable prefix it is no longer a martini), it may seem a little me-ish of me to turn around and walk all over the Bloody Caesar—but have you *had* a Gin Caesar? It's not like I'm suggesting ice cream or dog water as a substitute; I think the Gin Caesar as a variation that pays respect to its roots is legitimate, as legitimate as the vodka martini. While vodka trades in crispness and subtlety, the complex aromatics of gin can lend a depth and character to the drink that its imperial honorific has always implied.[1]

I toyed with the idea of renaming it, because such shifts as the substitution of the base spirit have certainly been cause for cocktail speciation in the past. "The Brutus" would have been cute, and all the more fitting if it happened to catch on, leaving its predecessor deposed and bleeding from twenty-three wounds on the steps of the senate. But who am I to entertain such thoughts? I didn't

---

1 Depending on the gin. I have not yet settled on what brand works best, but I eagerly look forward to trying it with Hendrick's, and maybe finally finding a use for this perplexing French saffron gin that I impulse-purchased at the Paris Duty Free last year, and has been sitting in my bar unattended to—like an olde-timey harlot with her makeup just a little off-puttingly askew. In any case, I'm sure they were using something predictable like Beefeater at the Toronto bar where I drank the five of these that won me over.

invent the damn thing, I just drink it. And even that I didn't do until my good friend Lee introduced me to it in the squalid and graffiti-stained booth of a Tex-Mex bar one post-New Year's Day breakfast.[2]

Like its cousin the Bloody Mary, the great strength of the Caesar, whether gin or vodka, is that it nourishes and revitalizes, and does the Bloody Mary one better by the protein contributed by the clam juice (I assume there is actually no protein in clam juice, but it makes for a good argument). Even the simplest of its garnishes, the celery stick, borders on being a snack itself, so thoroughly for the betterment of one's constitution is this drink designed. For these reasons, among others that remain obscure to me, it is one of the few cocktails (in such good company as the Mimosa, the Kir, and the Vermouth Cassis) that is truly acceptable to drink at breakfast time and throughout the day outside of the context of a lakeside cottage or gigantic mansion (if you live in a mansion, you can do whatever you want, whenever you want).

For all its charms, it is nonetheless with some chagrin that I express my admiration, for it was none too long ago that one of the key ingredients (if not *the* key ingredient) of the Caesar was the subject of my ignorant and impudent scorn. For years Clamato juice seemed to me the apogee of gastronomic impropriety—in exactly the vein of moralizing opprobrium that I have elsewhere disavowed,[3] I decried it as not only patently gross, but in some way "just plain

---

2 Given the inevitable resentment, regret, and hangover that characterizes New Year's Day, I have come to appreciate the value of January second as a better measure of how one is going to approach the dawning year. Thus it was on surer feet, fresh from an optimistic stride, that I sat down to what would prove to be quite an illuminating drink.
3 See "Not Much Pluck,"

wrong." A phrase that is in like company with patriotism and the *reductio ad Hitlerum* as the last refuges of the scoundrel and/or buffoon.

It is only with chagrin and not mortification that I own up to these sentiments because I tend to look upon my past excesses (as I intend to look upon my present excesses in the distant future) with an air of, "Oh, you rascally zealot, you!" A spirit of indulgence that I think is important if we are not to go around dying of embarrassment all the time.

When I write "ignorant", I refer not only to my ignorance of the deliciousness of Clamato juice, but also of its fine precedent. For what more delicious meeting of land and sea in Italian cuisine can be conjured than *spaghetti alle vongole*—spaghetti and clams, usually at its best in a garlicky sauce of white wine and tomatoes—a dish paralleled in its deliciousness only by the comical inconvenience of eating long pasta tossed with unshucked shellfish. It is a meal I cannot imagine consuming in either poor humour or extreme self-seriousness, and in this light Clamato seems no longer a peculiar aberration but a sort of natural descendent.

As the story goes, however, it was not in fact *spaghetti alle vongole* that inspired Clamato originally, but rather, and somewhat perplexingly, the desire to produce a beverage reminiscent of clam chowder (the clam chowder of my own youth was resolutely white, or at least beige, so I never would have surmised such an origin on my own). Where *spaghetti alle vongole* does come into play is in the invention of the Bloody Caesar, not a full year after Clamato hit the market in 1969, by Walter Schell of the Calgary hotel. At least he claims the dish as his inspiration, although it is unclear to me what, clam and tomato already being united in the Clamato itself, drove him to assemble the rest of the ingredients

(Worcestershire sauce, celery salt, tabasco and vodka, classi-cally), none of which have anything to do with *spaghetti alle vongole*. However, I certainly can't fault him for it.

At least *now* I can't. At one time I would have thought him a madman-and I cannot reduce that evaluation to my former strident veganism, for more than that I believe it betrays my roots as a Bad Islander. For aside from the nautical-grade beard I've proven myself capable of growing in recent years, a poorer specimen of a Maritimer you could not find. To think! Born on the West coast and raised on the East by natives of Sydney, Cape Breton and Pugwash, Nova Scotia, respectively, and I grew up with no particular love for the bounty of the sea, a poor internal compass, and only the faintest, most occasional trace of an accent. I don't even know how to swim. I am a great fan of *Moby Dick*, *Das Boot*, and H.P. Lovecraft's "The Shadow Over Innsmouth," but an uneasy romanticization of the sea and slight mistrust of its vastness ("frolic in brine, goblins be thine," they say) does not an Islander make.

In the spirit of making amends whilst supplying for my own gratification, however, I have very recently begun to savage the sea's rapidly dwindling resources with a perhaps ecologically unconscionable enthusiasm. Who could have known that mussels, the bright feather in my home prov-ince's cap, were so delicious? I abominated them for years based solely on my experiences as a dishwasher, having to routinely drain the twenty-gallon mussel buckets of what I am led to believe was their piss, and refresh their ice—a task which perhaps would not have irked me so had I any initial sympathy for them as a meal or for those who dined upon them. It is strange to come around on a deep-seated prejudice after so many years. It is similarly that I see my appreciation for Clamato juice (really only in Caesar form, I'll admit), although for whatever reason the cocktail stands as the bearer of greater symbolic import despite its estrangement from the actual form of the shellfish. The Caesar has become in its own way an emblem of my getting over both my aversion to shellfish and my petty bigotries about proper and unseemly food combinations.

You Wonder Why We're
Only Half Ashamed, Because
Enough is Too Much

But look around—can you blame us?

It hasn't come easy, and in fact I feel a little uneasy writing it even now. But I think I prefer the Reese's Big Cup to the regular peanut butter cup. Strange, no?

There has already been much spoken, and I imagine written, on the delicacy of the chocolate/peanut butter ratio of the Reese's Peanut Butter Cup, a balance upon which the entire success of the product rests (and on the disruption of which many spinoff products, such as the Inside Out Cup, have capsized) so I'll refrain from adding to that already ample body of discourse. At the risk of sounding iconoclastic, however, I think the Big Cup does it better.

I just now (circa last May), while craving a Big Cup specifically, forced myself to buy a package of regular sized cups in order to test my suspicions, and I feel fortunate that in doing so I have clarified somewhat the facts of the matter; there is something altogether too *fleeting* about the Regular Cup. Despite there being three to a package, they each and every one seem to be dispatched with unsatisfying quickness, leaving one with the sense that one could eat a whole other pack and be left in a state of dissatisfaction persisting, hand in hoof, with one's inevitably mounting nausea.

In contrast, the Big Cup borders on being perversely substantial. The peanut butter is really thick, *almost* off-puttingly so, and one thus has the time to truly register their teeth descending[1] through a pat of peanut butter of some heft and depth.

But its greatest strength lies in how the Big Cup proclaims its sheer excess, even before the first bite is taken. It is immediately disproportionate in several senses—of different proportions, chocolate to peanut butter, than the Regular Cup, but despite this it is comfortingly *in proportion* to itself, which is to say that it, you know, tastes good. But then in another sense it is *out* of proportion to *the world*—it is, in relation to the proper order of things, oversized, misshapen, and faintly grotesque; but still so close to the familiar as to render it that much more subtly disconcerting. Like one of those miniature Dobies (or maybe they're just Doberman-flavoured Chihuahuas); of slightly different proportions than a 'normal' sized Doberman, but while still retaining a certain sensibility in the parts' relationship to each other, unavoidably out of the ordinary in its relationship to the world, and thus unavoidably hilarious.

So just as the mini-Dobie is *strangely* too small, so is the Big Cup *strangely* too big; it is made strange—alienated—by its Bigness. In this alien encounter the usual circuit of understanding is disrupted. One asks oneself, "Is this magic?" "Can I eat this?" "What will happen?" and it is thus in its excess that the Big Cup becomes *enough*, and becomes truly satisfying, in contrast to the satisfaction deferred *in perpetuum* of the Regular Cup. It is *enough* because it is always already too much, somehow sidestepping "*more than enough*" entirely. And so it would be on its own,

---

1 Funny that we tend to think of our teeth as descending as we bite down on or into a substance, when since only our lower jaw is a mobile hinge, we are actually propelling our teeth upward into the food and pushing it against our stationary top teeth, like an unfortunate *Mortal Kombat* combatant uppercutted into a ceiling of spikes. Still, the semantic and somatic illusion persists. I wonder what came first, the idea or the sensation?

but of course it comes in packs of two, forcing one into that awkward position of it seeming inappropriate to eat both, but which one inevitably does.

I don't feel so good.

Boire Comme un Trou

Boire comme un trou, (Fr.) phrase to drink like a hole.

Something we picked up in Paris last winter (the saying, not the habit. Paris was merely where the habit began to grow a little shop-soiled and we considerably more self-hating for wear), which I'm sure means to drink to excess.

I like it because while pouring something down a hole implies a certain wastage, even a hole gets filled up at a certain point (that point I enjoy describing as my cup having runneth over). So let's be realistic; excess is all about acknowledging, if not abiding by, limits (good sense, stomach capacity, health), and so as far as toasts go, "*Ce soir, on boit comme un trou,*" or more casually "*Comme un trou!*" is pretty good.

Or, dispensing with affectation (assuming one is in the company of Anglophones): "Tonight, we drink like a hole."

> And with that the king saw coming toward him the strangest beast that ever he saw or heard of; so the beast went to the well and drank, *and the noise was in the beast's belly like unto the questing of thirty couple hounds; but all the while the beast drank there was no noise in the beast's belly; and therewith the beast departed with a great noise, whereof the king had great marvel*...Right sor there came a knight afoot unto Arthur and said...

"Tell me if you saw a strange beast pass this way."

'Such one I saw," said King Arthur, "that is past two mile; what would ye with the beast?" said Arthur.

"Sir, I have followed that beast long time, and killed mine horse, so would God that I had another to follow my quest... for I have followed this quest twelvemonth, and either I shall achieve him, or bleed of the best blood of my body."

Pellinore, that time king, followed the Questing Beast, and after his death Sir Palomides followd it.

–Sir Thomas Mallory, *Le Morte D'Arthur*,
Book I, Chapter 19

There's probably something to be learned here.

There Was No Pursuit
and No Seduction

From Graham Greene's *The End of The Affair* (1951):

The film was not a good film, and at moments it was acutely painful to see situations that had been so real to me twisted into the stock clichés of the screen...Suddenly and unexpectedly, for a few minutes only, the film came to life. I forgot that this was my story, and that for once this was my dialogue, and was genuinely moved by a small scene in a cheap restaurant. The lover had ordered steak and onions, the girl hesitated for a moment to take the onions, because her husband didn't like the smell, the lover was hurt and angry because he realized what was behind the hesitation, which brought to his mind the inevitable embrace on her return home. The scene "came off": I had wanted to convey the sense of passion through some common simple episode without any rhetoric in words or action, and it worked. For a few seconds I was happy—this was writing: I wasn't interested in anything else in the world. I wanted to go home and read the scene over: I wanted to work at something new: I wished, how I wished, that I hadn't invited Sarah Miles to dinner.

Afterwards—we were back at Rules and they

had just fetched our steaks—she said, 'There was one scene you *did* write."

"Yes."

"About the onions?"

"Yes." And at that very moment a dish of onions was put on the table. I said to her—it hadn't even crossed my mind that evening to desire her— "And does Henry mind onions?"

"Yes. He can't bear them. Do you like them?"

"Yes." She helped me to them and then helped herself.

Is it possible to fall in love over a dish of onions? It seems improbable and yet I could swear just then that I fell in love. It wasn't, of course, simply the onions—it was that sudden sense of an individual woman, of a frankness that was so often later to make me happy and miserable.[1]

---

1 It is more than ironic (or perhaps less? merely sad?) that this scene was not included in Edward Dmytryk's 1955 adaptation of the novel, not only because I find it one of the most effective of the book, but because it would have created such a clever little *mise en abîme*. Maybe, however, the weight was too much—if the scene did not play well on the screen it would be all the more tragic and compromising, threatening to indict the entire act of translation of the director. For his own part, Greene has expressed the almost inevitable dissatisfaction of seeing his writing adapted to film: "Why go through the unpopular motions of fighting every battle lost at the start? [The author] knows that even if a script be followed word for word there are those gaps of silence which can be filled with the banal embrace, irony can be turned into sentiment by some romantic boob of an actor..." ("The Novelist and the Cinema: A Personal Experience," 1958) I like to think that he is speaking here of *The End of the Affair*, which I found a tepid and uncompelling film; despite Deborah Kerr, whom I admire greatly for *Black Narcissus* and *The Innocents* (a great adaptation of James' *The Turn of the Screw*), but was not at all the Sarah Miles I had in mind when reading the novel; and *because of* Van Johnson, whose sad, uncomprehending face reminds me always and inexplicably of soured milk. Perhaps they were just unable to make the scene "come off."

I don't intend, of course, to comment on every literary food reference (literary reference to food) I happen to come upon, that would be a task both gargantuan and tiresome. But now and then, as in the above, one is struck, and the urge to share is irresistible.

I am a sucker for onions, and it seems to me that onions are a vegetable often undersung, for all their ubiquity.[2] This realization came to me all of a sudden, after years of waxing ecstatic over garlic (not by any means unworthy of such tribute), and it dawned on me that while I could live an admittedly impoverished Happy Life without garlic, no such life would be possible without onions. In fact, could I recall a single (cooked, non-dessert) meal I had prepared in my whole cookin' life that did not either commence or conclude with onions? At only the slimmest risk of hyperbole, *no*.

Thusly did onions emerge from the murk of the wings— essential but unnoticed—into the footlights of my affection.

So I approve their being given a central, if synecdochal[3] a role in Greene's book, however much "It wasn't, of course, simply the onions." Just as it was, and was not, simply *the bomb* that ended the affair. (I suddenly am having this flash of fervent curiosity as to whether Mor-

---

2 A notable and much appreciated exception, David Waltuck, of Chanterelle (NYC, RIP):

> You can't cook without onions. There is not a single thing you can do without onions. There are so many things made with onions that when people come into our restaurant and say that they are allergic to onions, I say, "No you are not—it is impossible. You just don't like onions." People eat onions all the time and don't know it. I remember having a conversation with Jasper Johns, with him saying, "If truffles and onions cost the same amount of money, you would obviously choose an onion. You don't need truffles; you do need onions."

A sentiment which, if pressed, I'm sure many cooks would echo, if less brassily.

rissey's "if it's not love, then it's the bomb the bomb the bomb that will bring us together" is in any way derived from *The End of the Affair*. Without getting into it, both Love and The Bomb play in complicated and not necessarily conflicting ways at the keeping together/driving apart of the two principal characters. This may not be such a stretch considering the wealth of English literary allusions that abound in Morrissey's songwriting. A familiarity with Greene's work is already (albeit a decade later) established by his reference to Greene's *Brighton Rock* (1938) on *Vauxhall And I*'s "Now My Heart Is Full.")

⚊

But this is not, all indications to the contrary, about my love for onions; rather, it is about *green peppers* and my extreme dislike for them. For it was while transcribing the above passage that I had the thought that steak with fried up onions and green peppers was perhaps the only situation in which I can imagine desiring green peppers. Not merely tolerate, but actively desire. Quite the thing, considering how much I fuckin' hate those guys. But did I always hate them?

I tell myself that one day (not too long ago) I "realized" that I Hate Green Peppers, which implies that the hatred

---

3 This is perhaps pushing it. How to describe the part-for-the-whole relationship of the onions to adultery in this situation? Synecdoche describes a part-standing-in-for-whole, subclass-for-class relationship, and vice versa, but I (and my English BA roommate) understand it usually be a more direct relationship. I do not know what better term to employ, and so will trust my gut that on an emotional register the decision to eat the onions is, as a minor betrayal, a subclass of the larger class of betrayals that will come to comprise their affair (including, among others, having sex on the floor of the sitting room while her husband is sick in bed upstairs). This decision also allows me to take advantage of the alliteration, for which the better angels of my nature apologize, and blame the pleasant weather/chirping birds or the cold I'm just getting over. Take your pick.

was always there, but I was somehow unaware of it, and it took someone articulating the thought (by saying, "I hate green peppers," or like "Green peppers are stupid and suck," or "Green peppers belong in Staten Island, with all the other trash," or something) for me to come to terms with what I was feeling all along.

It is a comforting thought, because it reaffirms the unity of the self and the continuity of identity—that life is a succession of peelings away of layers of artifice to arrive at the real, abiding self. I am, however, skeptical of such notions, or I harbour a healthy pessimism, at least.

It's difficult to say, because I had a long stint of eating them, you know, pretty much all the time, owing to their status as the "Second Vegetable" of vegetarianism. It seems that for the first years of most people's vegetarianism, green peppers have a way of popping up in pretty much everything, more for a lack of better ideas of what to put in a dish, I would argue, than out of anyone's genuine enthusiasm for them. In fairness, this is a consequence of their versatility combined with a general lack of imagination on the part of many non- or recently vegetarian cooks. Carrots and potatoes take too long to cook, broccoli has an unwieldy shape, and pretty much everything else costs too much or eighty percent of people don't know how to cook it.

I'm generalizing, obviously, but I am certain that many white or whiteish middle class vegetarian or ex-vegetarian punks (or not. It's cool) will sympathize with this experience, particularly if their entry into the lifestyle roughly corresponded with a) their adolescence, and b) their learning how to cook.

It is just, for many people, the first (next) vegetable that comes to mind, and so it survives by stinking up stir-frys, pizzas, and pasta salads the land over, inexplicable but omnipresent. Insinuating itself quietly into the company of onions and garlic for the initial sauté...

What, for example, is on your average vegetarian pizza? Onions (the First Vegetable, despite my arguments about their anonymity, but they are still clearly taken for granted), tomatoes (which don't count, because they're a fruit), and what, olives? Two kinds of olives? Which I argue don't count either because everyone, if they think about it, will realize that they've always secretly and unconsciously—clandestine even unto themselves—considered olives a fruit. Or maybe part condiment? In any case not a full-fledged vegetable. Try it, you'll see. And lo, green peppers, which suck.

So, all that time, all those fledgling years, was I really labouring blind, under the half-felt, inarticulable but loathsome influence of green peppers? For they *are* foul, tasting at best like batteries and grass-flavoured bubble gum (if there was such a thing), or, if you are so unfortunate as to miss this dubious window, like something always already a little rotten.

Or am I just embarrassedly projecting my current revulsion, the putrefying metal I imagine now on my tongue, into a past to which it cannot presume truthfully to belong? Am I just ruining it for myself? Interceding in my own memories in order to shore up this fiction of a unitary self, and affect forged membership with the cache of those who always were aware of the shabby interloping of green peppers into otherwise edible cuisine?

Well, I guess we'll never know.

(I might eat a stuffed pepper, actually. Stuffed with lentils? Yeah, maybe.)

God Help Me

I saw an old photo recently of a friend as a young punk, perched behind a Food Not Bombs banner, and it got me thinking about my life as a... whatever it is that I am. A person who cares about and is interested in food. I hesitate to use the term "foodie" not only because I dislike it, but because for purposes of retrospection it certainly cannot describe my relationship to food before the cultural moment at which "foodie" became a salient term. I have written elsewhere about my discomfort with the term, and while I have no problem at all with people self-describing as such, I am put off by how the label rarifies something so universal and essential to life by reinscribing it as a *lifestyle*. I do not mean to claim that I am any less precious or annoying or of the present time by insisting that I am not a foodie, but simply someone who is very interested in food, but I do not feel that I profit much from so identifying. I am also aware that the term is of only slightly more recent vintage than myself (coined by Barr & Levy in their 1984 *The Official Foodie Handbook*), and like myself, had as its aim to circumvent some of the pretence and stuffiness of the gourmet, but hell, I am an obstinate bastard, so let's leave it at that.

Really a more relevant question which arises is whether "my life as a foodie" (nominal anachronism aside) is actually something that exists. Can a trajectory be described that takes me from Food Not Bombs to duck fat, mussels, and scotch club? I often dig pretty far into my past when I write about food, and I have been asked more than once how I got into food and cooking, but I have never had an answer ready at hand. Admittedly, the above FNB to Audacious Glutton trajectory is not so hard to trace. I never played a major role with Food Not Bombs, but I consider it central to framing how I thought about food, or perhaps more to the point, setting up food as something to be thought about, as opposed to merely consumed. There was no chapter in Prince Edward Island, despite the numerous attempts to found one, and so I was best familiar with the Halifax Food Not Bombs. I don't recall whether I found FNB through my friends, or stumbled into new friendships through the medium of shared free food (it doesn't much matter), but several of the people involved were some of the first "good cooks" I met; ironically, maybe, given the connotations of food either over- or under-seasoned which plague so many free-food operations.

Of course, FNB could also be seen as but part of a larger development in my relationship to food—that of becoming first vegetarian, then vegan shortly thereafter. If you've ever spent any time with vegans, you know that food is a huge part of their social reality: eating food, preparing food, sharing recipes, tales of amazing vegan edibles in far flung cities or previously overlooked eateries, or merely commiserating, thrown together as they are by the common experiences of a life of perpetual vigilance, ingredient-scrutinizing, social awkwardness, and tacit exclusion by the better part of the tables of the world.[1] Veganism in general and Food Not Bombs in particular certainly served an indispensable purpose in providing a foundation, beyond punk, partying, and beards when I was loafing around San Francisco

---

1 This situation has changed somewhat over the years, of course, as veganism gains in popularity and recognition.

hungry and doe-eyed some years later.

But this gets beyond the question of origins, of turning points. Just about any chef or foodie memoir one picks up these days will somewhere contain an account of the author's gastronomic awakening, whether in the sepia-toned days of their youth or crucially late in the game. I do not doubt the veracity or honesty of such seminal experiences, but, as narratively compelling as they are I cannot point to a pivotal moment when my heart first sank into my stomach, there to remain, and I felt my soul thenceforth yoked to the unholy mill of my appetites. My relationship to food has been, one might say, sufficiently overdetermined as to confound attempts to trace the origins of the harried and hungry creature that I have become. My parents were hippies, or something rather nearer to the aftershock of the hippies, a little less radical, a little less back to the land (they lived for a while, I'm told, in a tiny house on top of a hill, a derelict farm in Avonlea that they quitted before I was born), but growing up there was still in my house homemade yoghurt and granola, "natural" peanut butter, a moratorium on pro- cessed, "bought'n" food (it in fact took some years of grade school humiliation to train me out of the habit of referring to all non-home baked cookies as "bought'n cookies"), and a garden behind. My mother was reputedly the first Islander to strong-arm the local health food store into importing tofu in from the mainland, and in a manner almost startling for how it would foreshadow my Submission Hold-devoted adolescence,[2] always insisted that if she got her hands on a button-maker she would make herself a "It's Garlic" button

---

2 How many stick 'n' poke tattoos have been inspired by the *Garlic For Victory* seven-inch we may never know. Or we could take everyone who has a home-done garlic tattoo, and subtract from that the number of them who never listened to Submission Hold and that will give us a pretty good idea.

that she could wear to head off any olfactory awkwardness she should encounter out in polite company.

Mary (my brother and I have always called our parents by their first names, it continues to feel strangely impersonal to refer to her as "my mother," however indelibly she was that) played a somewhat unconventional role in my culinary tutelage. The combination of her ailing health and the dietary experimentation undertaken to combat her illness meant that she rarely had the time or energy to cook for the family, and rarer still was she eating the same fare as ourselves. With my father working and my brother having flown the coop to university it very quickly fell to me to take on a share of the dinner duties. For all the years that I cooked for my family I can honestly only remember making three dishes: Hunter's Delight, tuna casserole, and something that can only legitimately be taken as a variation upon the second, or even a combination of the two.

Hunter's Delight was ground beef sautéed up with onions and green peppers, made into a sauce with chili powder, (and probably, what? Garlic powder, oregano, basil?), a can of tomato soup, and mixed with rotini pasta. I realize now that it was effectively the same basic result as the Hamburger Helper that all my slightly better- or slightly worse-off (it's hard to tell what is symbolized with packaged foods like that) friends were eating, but I am inclined to think that it (usually) tasted better, and I am happy to have a sort of muscular memory of all of the white-capped brown glass jars that our dried herbs and spices were kept in, and that my mother kept an inexhaustible supply of.

Tuna casserole consisted of broad egg noodles tossed with a sauce of cream of mushroom soup, canned tuna, and peas. At no point did a casserole dish come into play in this meal; but it was customary, and arguably the best part, that a handful of plain potato chips be crushed up on top the steaming noodles before serving. Chips, in fact, were the one undeniably "junk" food that had a place in our house as far back as I can remember, and I certainly got the run of my money with tuna casserole as a chip-bearing vessel, so much so that I recall at one point being told that I could not make the dish once more until the family had a few solid weeks of other kinds of food.

The third dish was just the tuna casserole, but made with ground beef in lieu, no chips, and I think a dollop of yoghurt thrown in, and may have had some humble pretensions to beef stroganoff. It was pretty good. I realize now there were other things that I must have made; tuna salad sandwiches (with chunks of apple, motherfucker, don't doubt) and tomato soup; hotdogs on brown bread, cooked in the toaster oven so that they blistered and split open their leathery, almost-animal skin; or sloppy joes, also on brown bread, that one would be hard-pressed to distinguish from hunter's delight sans pasta, except that the spice would be amped up slightly, maybe with some orange cheddar for good measure.

This arrangement was only interrupted when I got my first job, a dishpig in a restaurant/bar, which provided me with or served as the backdrop for many other memorable moments (First Time I Got My Hand Covered With Maggots, First Time I Enjoyed Mushrooms, First Time I Felt Physically Angry At Mussels, First Time I Obscured My Tears In The Steam of a Dishwasher[3]), and also effectively removed me from the routinized meal-economy of our household. I can look back now and realize that my begin-

---

3 See "Can Ye Never Go Home," "*Et Tu*"

ning work in the restaurant industry may have ushered in the end of what remained of family dinners in our household. The practice never quite recovered in the years to follow, whether I was working or not, for it was dealt another blow by the disruption of my vegetarianism. Family togetherness aside, it was simply not practical for three people to attempt to prepare three different meals at the same time on one stove, and so outside of special occasions or truly concerted efforts at coordination, we began to drift through a kitchen that was no longer a hub, but at best a place of transitory and occasionally overlapping feedings. There was much grazing in those days.

I once got it into my head that no one should be allowed to eat in a restaurant unless they had spent some time in a dish pit, and while I am no longer so filled with righteous ire against the dining set, I (and Orwell with me) continue to think it would do the world a world of good. While life-lessons and unfortunate forays into the darker depths of one's personality are *de rigueur* when working in a kitchen, I managed to learn little in the way of technique in the years it took me to work my way up from dishwasher to line cook (although I did succeed in starting a number of fires), and honestly neither did my palate or proclivities undergo any appreciable refinement. One night it dawned on me that a person who had only restaurant experience behind him would, past a certain age, be hard-pressed to find work elsewhere, and all it took was one day looking around at the savaged personalities and unsettling glints in the eyes of my coworkers and a bit of mental calculus to see if I could survive a life path trodden through such pitiless country. It reminds me of a doctor I once heard speaking of working long stints in the

Antarctic. "The first time you do it for adventure," he said, "the second time you do it for money."

"The third," he concluded, "You do it because you can't function anywhere else anymore."

So I quit. More than that, I vowed that night to never work in a kitchen again. I prefer to reserve such a half-mad glint for when I am sitting down to a well-laden table, rather than when I am sharpening a large knife or subconsciously and automatically re-wringing a sweat-soaked bandana while attempting to recognize the contours of my face in a not particularly reflective stainless-steel cooler door.

That was a good many years ago, and there's not a whole lot of obvious portent that has happened to me in the meantime, but I can safely say that I've damn well eaten my way through the intervening years with an unruly devotion that apparently has impressed itself on those around me, at least to the extent that they suggested I start writing about it in the perhaps vain hope that it might spare them having to listen to me talk about food so much of the time. Poor, dumb bastards.

And maybe that's it, looking back over such a CV one might ask how could it be otherwise? Steeped in food and cooking as necessary, quotidian, but always considered; then professionalized; then further rendered conspicuous anew, as a social matrix and a political provocation; it seems inevitable that I should end up, at this moment in time, grudgingly but legibly a "foodie" (grumble). Does it not? As such I can ingenuously respond to the question of How I Got Into Food with "How could I not? I mean, I eat it like, *all the time*." What is missing is precisely that sense of the accidental, the indispensable, that lends both poetry and gravity to the gastronomical awakening. There is for me no

First Oyster or Summer Strawberry or even _____ That Grandma Used To Make that forever altered the path of my life and put me on the low road through the valley of the shadow of gourmandizing excess.

Here I stand, for I can do no other?

Acknowledgements

Sincere thanks to my editors Nic Boshart and Emily Horne, who have been as patient and indulgent as could be deemed editorially sound. I owe a debt to Hal Ferris and Zac Campbell, on whose computers I wrote much of the original material for this book. Thanks also to Greg Boone, who suggested I start writing in the first place.

An Index of Select Terms

INVISIBLE PUBLISHING is committed to working with writers who might not ordinarily be published and distributed commercially. We work exclusively with emerging and under-published authors to produce entertaining, affordable books.

We believe that books are meant to be enjoyed by everyone and that sharing our stories is important. In an effort to ensure that books never become a luxury, we do all that we can to make our books more accessible.

We are collectively organized and our production processes are transparent. At Invisible, publishers and authors recognize a commitment to one another, and to the development of communities which can sustain and encourage storytellers.

If you'd like to know more please get in touch.
info@invisiblepublishing.com

Invisible Publishing
Halifax & Toronto